Accelerate Your Learning

The Action Handbook

Colin Rose and Louise Goll

Designed, Developed and Published by

Accelerated Learning Systems Ltd.
50 Aylesbury Road
Aston Clinton
Aylesbury
Buckinghamshire
England

Written by

Colin Rose and **Louise Goll**

First Published 1992

ISBN 0 905553 40 3

Typeset and Layout by

Anna-Maria Blank

Cartoons by

Mick Davis

Printed and bound by

UNWIN BROTHERS LIMITED
The Gresham Press, Old Woking, Surrey
A Member of the Martins Printing Group

Acknowledgements

Some of the influences on this programme are obvious – they are mentioned in the text. There are other influences we wish to acknowledge explicitly.

We are particularly indebted to the work of Howard Gardner and his colleagues at Harvard University on Multiple Intelligences. It is a concept that should profoundly influence the future of teaching, training and learning.

We are also indebted to Arthur Costa for the work on learning preferences at California State University. We acknowledge, too, the work of Noel Entwistle at Edinburgh University on study skills and learning techniques.

The recommended reading list will indicate many further influences. Every one of the books is worth reading by anyone interested in the subject of learning.

Finally we appreciated the highly constructive and continuous support of John Greenacre, Chris Handley, John Giles and our colleagues Diana Rose and Steve Minshull.

Inspiration and common sense insight have a major part to play in any undertaking of this nature. Dee Dickinson provided the one — Keith Newman of Rover Learning Business provided the other, during an earlier project.

Thanks!

Colin Rose & Louise Goll — September 1992

Contents

Stage ONE – Getting into the right state of mind

Stage TWO – Get the facts to suit yourself

Stage THREE – Explore the subject

Stage THREE – Continued . . .

Stage FOUR – Memorise the key facts

Stage FIVE – Show you know

Stage SIX – Reflect on how you learned

Just Open Your Mind

Consider these two pictures. The picture on the right was drawn by the same person as the one on the left after just one hour of instruction!*

The person who learned to draw so well so quickly, was a 64 year old grandmother.

The techniques to improve how you learn are universal. That's why this Handbook works for students in full time education and adults at work and at home.

Like so many of us that person had believed "I can't draw". Yet one hour later she could draw a portrait to be proud of.

What had happened in that one hour?

The instructor had freed her from the self-imposed belief that she "Could not draw". The ability was there all the time.

All the teacher did was to release that ability. The student then began to develop on her own towards her real potential. She was not working harder, but she was now working smarter.

We can all draw when we are shown how. We can all learn well, when we are shown how. The choice then is ours. Too often past disappointments with learning cause us to create needless barriers and put artificial limits on ourselves.

Yet, when we understand the process of learning, we can start to reach our true potential.

Even people who have already shown themselves to be successful learners have "blind spots" – areas they feel unsure about. Mathematics and foreign languages are typical areas. Learning how to learn helps eliminate those blind spots, and ensure you are learning with maximum effectiveness.

Someone who is an effective learner controls his or her life. To wait to be taught makes you dependent on someone else. When you control your own learning, you are independent. You literally do have the key to your own future.

* The instruction was a self-study programme called "Yes . . .You **can** draw". It's available from the address at the back of this manual.

What Works For You?

Below are five common learning situations. You probably have experienced most, perhaps all of them. Think back to the times when you were asked to learn something by **each** of these methods.

Then write down what seemed to make learning effective for you in each of these situations.

From a book or manual	From a lecture, or talk from teachers, experts or instructors	From a practical training session which includes hands on activities	From a training video	From a colleague or fellow student

ACTION

Looking back at your answers, which situations seemed to work best? Which did you enjoy? Is there a pattern, or any common elements in the way you learn best? Things that make learning work well for you?

What works for other people?

We asked 100 people: here are some of the things that made learning effective for them.

From a book or manual	From a lecture	From a training session that includes hands on activities	From a training video	From a colleague or fellow student
Stopping often to check if I really understood it. Making notes in my own words. Highlighting – underlining key ideas. Looking for similar comparisons. Reading difficult bits out loud.	Asking questions. Making notes of key ideas. Make a check list of important ideas. Comparing notes afterwards with a friend.	Making a diagram or drawing. Answering questions. Doing case histories. Solving problems.	Stopping every now and then to jot down what I learned. Discussing it afterwards. Pausing the tape to note down points I wanted to ask about.	Discussing the ideas with others. Getting their reaction to my ideas. Comparing notes.

What does not work?

When we asked 100 people what they considered poor ways to learn, they included answers like:

- Reading a boring text book.
- Just sitting watching a video, without the chance to discuss it afterwards.
- Listening to a lecture, without making notes or without discussing it.
- Reading for an hour or more without stopping to think about the subject or make notes.
- Just copying things down without thinking about them.
- Just chatting to friends without a clear aim of what we were trying to achieve.
- Daydreaming and doodling.

ACTION

Look at what works and what does not seem to work. What is the essential difference? Make up your mind before you turn the page!

You Only Learn By Taking Action!

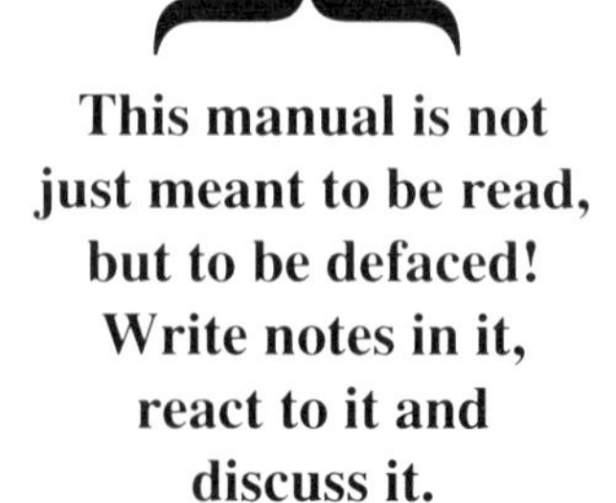

This manual is not just meant to be read, but to be defaced! Write notes in it, react to it and discuss it.

"The only truly educated person is the one who has learned how to learn."

Carl Rogers
Educational Psychologist

You learn with your brain and your brain is as individual as your fingerprints. So this programme cannot give you a fixed formula which, like a magic pill, will automatically guarantee to turn you into a super learner overnight.

What it can do – which is much more valuable – is let you discover for yourself the steps **you** need to take in order to become a highly competent learner.

But there is a price to pay if you are to discover your own personal plan for success. You will not be able to sit passively and merely read this book. You will have to answer the questions, and do the exercises.

On many pages of this Handbook you will see the word "ACTION". This is where you need to **do** something if you really are to discover about yourself and the ways you learn best.

Maybe the single biggest difference between good and poor learners is the extent to which they **explore** the subject i.e. get actively involved. The image of learning has tended to be of someone reading quietly, or sitting passively listening to a teacher.

For most people, and most situations, that image is completely wrong!

Effective learning involves asking questions, talking aloud, drawing, moving, arguing, discussion, music ... and fun.

If you work through this Handbook you will have transformed a surface knowledge of the six stages of learning into a deep understanding of how **you** learn best. You will discover for yourself what works. You will, therefore, believe in the programme.

One further point. Some of the ideas are simple and the reasons for using them are obvious. Other ideas require more explanation and exploration. That's what this Handbook will achieve.

Find out what best suits you – and what best suits different situations

But will you really pay the price?

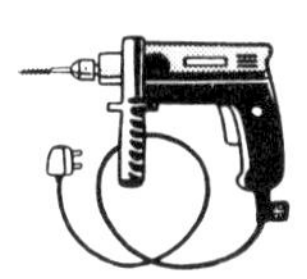

There is always a "cost" to any human endeavour – either in terms of money, effort or working now for a reward in the future.

There's a useful way to assess how ready you are to pay that cost. It's often called a cost/benefit analysis. You wrote down some benefits when you answered the initial question "What's In It For Me?"

There are two headings below. We've included some benefits of learning-to-learn. We have also included some "cost" or sacrifices you can expect to make. Add your own costs and benefits.

Ever felt overwhelmed by a learning task?

Join the club, we all have! This Handbook will help.

The costs

- ✗ Wading through this "Handbook"!
- ✗ Giving up precious leisure time, for a future benefit.
- ✗ Working through the exercises.
- ✗ Trying out the ideas.
- ✗ Giving up the excuse that some things are beyond me!
- ✗ Having a greater expectation of myself.

The Benefits

- ✓ Being able to learn new subjects quicker and with less effort.
- ✓ Being able to meet and master rapid change.
- ✓ Having skills I can pass on to my family.
- ✓ Enjoy a more varied leisure time.
- ✓ Pride and confidence in a key ability.
- ✓ Justify a higher income.

*This Handbook also helps you get the best out of books. And books are a key way to get the world's best minds to answer **your** questions.*

Other costs:

✗ . . . .

✗ . . . .

✗ . . . .

Other benefits

✓ . . . .

✓ . . . .

✓ . . . .

Only **you** can decide that you will pay the "price" and make the commitment.

Once you **are** sure that the benefits are worth the cost, you will have increased your motivation significantly.

Dr. Benjamin Bloom has spent a lifetime studying excellence.

His conclusion is that anyone can learn anything – the only difference is that some take more time than others.

If this programme helps with the rest of your life, it doesn't matter if it takes six days, six weeks or six months to complete. Does it?

Learn – With A Little Help From Your Friends

"Two heads are better than one." In learning to learn this is often true. So throughout *Accelerate Your Learning* we encourage you to use the support of others to help you to learn. For example :

- Pair up with somebody who wants to learn with you – get yourself a "Study Buddy".
- Enlist a friendly ear to allow you to think aloud, and sort out your thoughts.
- Discuss and swap ideas about learning with workmates or fellow students.

A great deal of research shows that learning in co-operation with others **increases our ability to learn well**. Why do you think learning in co-operation with others:

- Boosts achievement?
- Speeds up learning?
- Improves memory?
- Makes you feel more enthusiastic about learning?

"I learned not from those who taught, but from those who talked with me."

St. Augustine

ACTION

YOUR ANSWERS/THOUGHTS

Here's our reasons

1. When you learn with others, you have to discuss, explore and explain what you have learned. That very soon shows you whether or not you have really understood the subject.

   When you keep thoughts in your own head without expressing them out loud, it's all too easy to be "woolly". But when you have to explain them to other people, you need to think carefully, understand what it all means and organise your thoughts properly.

2. When you learn with others, you will be repeating what you know out loud. So you'll not just be reading it (**seeing**), but explaining it (**saying**) and you'll probably also be sketching things out or demonstrating things (**doing**).

   You will also be listening to other people's ideas and interpretations (**hearing**). In other words you will be **seeing**, **saying**, **hearing** and **doing**.

   According to some research, that combination of activities enables us to remember 90% of what we learn. And learning with friends, (or co-operative learning) can achieve this.

We remember up to 90% of what we see, say, hear and do.

Tackle learning with a friend and increase your chances of remembering what you learn.

Conclusion

Learning to seek out and use the support of others is an essential learning skill. The person who helps can be your official teacher, manager, supervisor or coach. It can also be your workmate or colleague, partner, friend or member of your family.

You not only begin to understand the subject better, you also see the different ways that other people tackle it.

Try a learning action circle

Here's an idea that works. Set up an informal learning action circle with some colleagues or friends who are also doing this programme. Compare notes and see how differently you all learn best.

Co-operative learning is such an important skill that we have a whole section on it in the supplement entitled "Six Super Skills".

What Are You Good At Now?

There are five headings below. Think of the things you are good at under **each** heading.

	Skills you learned before school	An academic or school subject	A skill that's useful in a work situation	A skill that's useful in a social/home situation	A hobby or sport
I'M GOOD AT THESE THINGS					
SOME TYPICAL ANSWERS	• A whole language. • How basic things work. • To walk, run, jump, climb. • The beginning of counting, the alphabet and even reading some words. • Dressing. • Painting.	• English. • Geography. • Maths. • A foreign language. • History. • Science. • Art. • Design technology. • Spelling. • Literature. • Cookery. • Religious studies.	• Negotiating. • Metalworking. • Typing. • Planning. • Letter writing. • Woodworking. • Selling. • Supervising. • Designing. • Figure work. • Getting on with other people.	• Parenting. • Putting people at ease. • Being a good friend. • Being a good partner. • Cooking. • Housekeeping. • Budgeting. • Explaining things clearly. • Listening.	• Gardening. • Football. • Art. • Knitting. • Tennis. • Reading. • D.I.Y. • Music.

Have you considered before that **all** these activities involve learning? The skill of learning has much broader applications than simply for "academic type" subjects. Academic type subjects are – for most people – purely the foundations on which they build other more directly "useful" skills. But because they are foundation skills they are vital.

Are you surprised at how many things you are competent at? They all involve learning. That's why you can apply the skills you learn here to hobbies and your whole life.

How did you become good at it?

Look back at the answers you've just given to the question "What are you good at?"

Now answer the question "How did you become good at them?"

YOUR ANSWER

I became good at the things I do well by:

____

____

____

____

____

What can you conclude?

You are **already** a very good learner. You have to be! No-one is born being able to talk, walk, budget for a family, count, build relationships, manage people, run a machine, drive a car, read a paper etc., etc.

"Ah ha", you say "but that sort of learning isn't the problem. It's the sort of learning that involves text books, lectures, computers and training rooms that's the challenge."

That is the heart of the issue.

Look back at the previous page. Most of our learning is **informal** learning. It's based on exploration and we do it pretty successfully. Indeed, many of the **most** important things of life are learned informally.

Formal learning requires some training

We have seen that informal learning is natural and successful.

By "informal" we mean:

- Discussing with others.
- Asking lots of questions.
- Trial and error, experimenting.
- Getting other people's reactions.
- Watching and practising.
- Having some fun.

The pre-school child learns like this. She uses all her senses, she's unstressed, she has individual attention, she's encouraged continuously – and she learns faster than at any other time of her life.

"Formal" learning requires some training. But we normally do not receive that training.

Many "adult" skills are also learned in a similar way. Through trial and error, talking to others, and asking questions.

It's the "formal" learning that tends to give us the problems.

Why? Because formal learning does not come naturally to many people. It is largely based on text books, lectures and study methods, and we need to be taught how to do it.

It's natural, for example, to dance. But you need some training to be able to do a "formal" dance, like a quickstep or a waltz.

Informal learning is natural

Informal learning is natural

It's the formal learning that you need to be trained for

The mistake we make

"Adults are really children with big bodies."

Bob Pike

Pre-school, (and Primary school children), learn with love and encouragement, they explore, they learn through games and they work on co-operative projects involving lots of different activities. It's fast, effective and fun.

Then the "rules" change. There is a sharp divide. We now sit in rows, we learn as individuals, we are taught differently and in more limited ways.

Funny thing – it doesn't seem to work as well!

We make a mistake when we assume that people mysteriously change how they learn best just because they are students – or adults. They don't. The elements that make for success for informal learning, make for success in formal learning.

Why is "Formal" Learning more difficult?

We think there are three reasons:

1. **It concentrates on books and lectures. These methods are effective and are necessary. But by themselves they are not enough for many people.**

   Many people – as we'll see – do not learn well unless they can **add** more natural ways to learn to the conventional and formal methods of teaching.

   Accelerate your Learning will show you how to add more natural ways to learn.

2. **Many books and lectures are written in a step–by–step, and "academic" style. That style often appears artificial and boring.**

   There's no point in saying that we shouldn't feel bored. Neither is there any point in saying we should "grin and bear it". You feel what you feel.

   The answer is not to grin and bear it, but to find ways of tackling this formal type of learning situation – and make it work for you.

3. **Most formal education requires us to work in large groups.**

   This reduces the amount of individual attention which is such a successful feature of most informal learning. The pre-school child usually has the individual attention of his parents and/or another caring adult. The worker normally has the individual attention of his boss and colleagues as he or she trains.

Ironically, whilst formal education usually involves large classes, the actual work we do is mostly on our own.

Yet interaction with other people improves both the quality and enjoyment of learning.

Why does this matter?

For a very important reason. Most people equate learning with formal, "study-type" learning.

Because they were never taught **how** to learn from books, lectures and training sessions, many people lack confidence in their ability in formal learning. Then they conclude, quite wrongly, that they are poor learners.

Others who can learn effectively in formal situations, do not necessarily enjoy it. They accept that they have to grin and bear it.

SELF-FULFILLING PROPHESIES

If you tell a golfer to make sure he doesn't hit the ball in the sand he probably will. If someone worries about their health they often make themselves ill.

Dr. Rosenthal in California told teachers he had measured the IQ of a class, and gave the teachers two lists. One group, he said, were the "bright" children, the other group were poor learners. In fact there was absolutely no difference between the two groups, and the teachers were instructed not to treat them differently.

Nevertheless, eight months later the group labelled "bright" had 28% better results than the second group.

Not one word had been said. Yet the teachers, quite unconsciously, had managed to communicate a higher expectation of the first group, and a lower expectation of the second. The students performed to this unspoken expectation.

We act according to what we believe to be true. And many of those beliefs stem from the images of ourselves that are stored in our brain. ***These images may not be true!***

How you behave is based on what you believe

What you have just read explains why some people feel negative about their school experience. If they are adults, they look back and **feel** a lack of confidence. If they are still students, they stop trying. Or they pretend that the subject is "stupid" or "irrelevant".

Such people probably needed more ways to explore the subject than was normally available. The way they were taught didn't match the way they needed to learn.

Result? They came to feel that they are poor learners. If they **feel** they are poor learners, they will come to **believe** they are poor learners. And if they believe they are poor learners, they will **behave** as poor learners. They avoid the issue, and deny themselves the chance to progress.

It's a vicious circle. A self-fulfilling prophesy. It puts such people off school and learning, sometimes for life.

Of course there are also many who **do** succeed very well in the conventional school system. **That's because the way schools usually teach fits the way their brains work.**

Even if you are already confident about your ability to learn, this programme will add **dozens** of tried and tested ideas to improve your effectiveness **and enjoyment in learning**. It will also help people who were less suited by conventional education, to break out of the vicious circle we have just identified. Because your attitude of mind makes a **big** difference to your success.

If you expect to succeed, you probably will.

You Have Got What It Takes!

More has been learned about the human brain in the last 15 years, than in all previous human history.

What we have learned can revolutionise education. But it has not yet! Which is why this programme can make such a significant contribution to you and your family.

ARE YOU BEING ACTIVE?
OR
ARE YOU BEING PASSIVE?

Active learners will be reading this with a pencil in their hand. Ready to jot down questions and do the exercises!

Your brain is an incredibly complex and capable piece of equipment – but it comes without an owner's manual. Rarely are we told how it works, and how to get the best out of it.

It is rather like having a super computer, but without all the programmes to make it work properly. Think of this course as providing some of the missing programmes.

Let us start by having a brief look at the "hardware" Your brain.

Three brains in one

The first surprise is that you actually have three brains. Each one evolved after the other.

At the base of your skull you have a rather primitive brain. It keeps you breathing and it keeps your heart beating. It tells you to fight or run when danger threatens. It also controls some of your more primitive instincts, like your sense of territory. Which is why you start feeling angry or uncomfortable when someone moves too close to you.

PRIMITIVE BRAIN

Next to evolve was your middle brain, a type of brain that mammals also possess. Only recently have we realised how important this mid-brain is to learning.

Your middle brain controls your hormonal system, your health (immune system), your sexuality, your emotions and an important part of your long term memory. The fact that our emotions and our long term memory are **both** controlled from this same middle brain, explains something we have all observed.

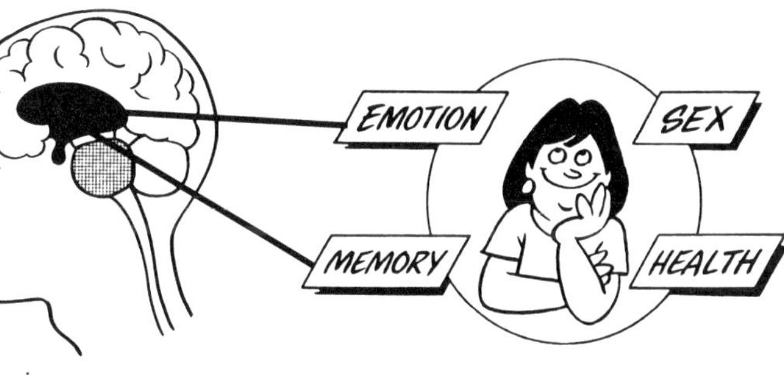

MIDDLE BRAIN

When something involves strong emotions, it is usually very well remembered. You probably remember your first kiss, for example? Or where you were when you heard someone significant had died. It also means enjoyment and fun are important elements in learning, because they involve positive emotions.

*Let's get your brain capacity into perspective. As it grows in the womb, a 12 week old human embryo is developing about 2,000 brain cells **a second**.*

An adult bee – which can do some pretty sophisticated things like building a honeycomb, calculating distances, and signalling the direction of pollen to its companions – has a total of about 7,000 brain cells or neurons.

That's the number of brain cells that a human embryo grows in about 3 seconds!

Dr. Paul MacLean is the scientist most identified with the idea of the brain in three parts. He calls it "The Triune Brain Theory".

Make a fist with your hand. Now wrap your other hand over the top of this fist. If your wrist represents your primitive brain, and the fist is your middle brain, the hand wrapped over it represents your new brain.

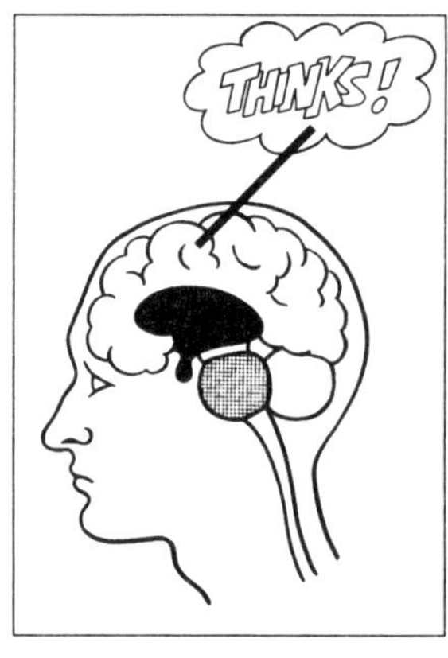

THINKING BRAIN

This third brain is truly extraordinary.

The good news is that this brain has **all** the capacity you will ever need to learn and remember anything you want. So long as you know how!

The incredible capacity of the brain has only recently been realised. You have about 100 **billion** brain cells. A number that is almost impossible to visualise. It is twenty times the entire population of the world.

A brain cell looks a bit like a miniature octopus. The cell is in the middle. Branching out from it are tiny threads. Each time something reaches one of your senses (sight, sound, or touch), it creates a thought or impression that travels out from a brain cell and along one of the little branch like threads. (These threads are called "dendrites" from a Greek word meaning branch).

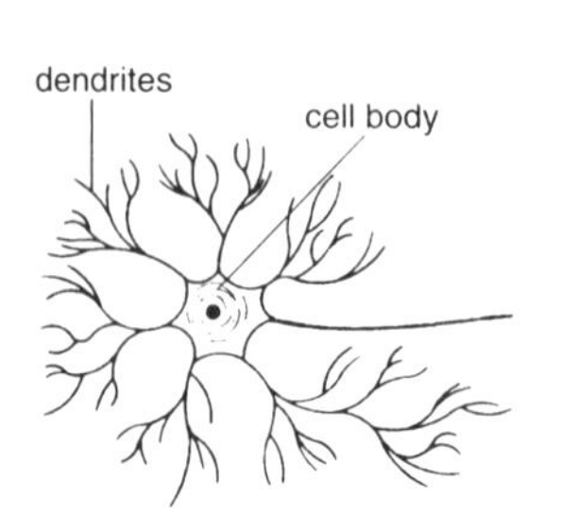

BRAIN CELL

Then the thought crosses over to another brain cell, via its "branch". The process continues with perhaps thousands or millions of brain cells being connected up in sequence. A split second mental chain reaction conducted by electrical activity.

Each time this chain reaction takes place, new connections are formed between brain cells. Some of these connections are permanent. That is why you can remember so many things without conscious effort, (like riding a bike).

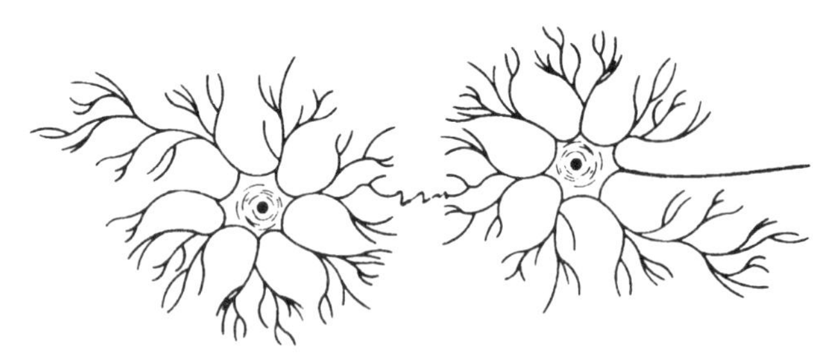

TWO BRAIN CELLS CONNECTING

Here is the significance. It is not really the number of brain cells you have, it is the number of connections you make between those brain cells that determines how "useful" your brain becomes, i.e. how intelligent you are.

The big news from brain scientists over the last 10–15 years is that intelligence is not fixed. We become more intelligent the more we use our brains, and the more stimulation we give our minds. Because the more you use your brain, the more connections you make between your brain cells. The more connections between your brain cells, the greater is your potential for intelligent thought.

You literally expand your brain through use. In a real sense you are the architect of your own brain. You can develop your **own** intelligence.

Barring injury or major illness, you do **not** lose brain capacity as you grow older, so long as you keep learning and keep seeking new experiences – through hobbies, reading, work, sports, art, music, etc. The brain thrives on novelty, and only declines with lack of stimulation.

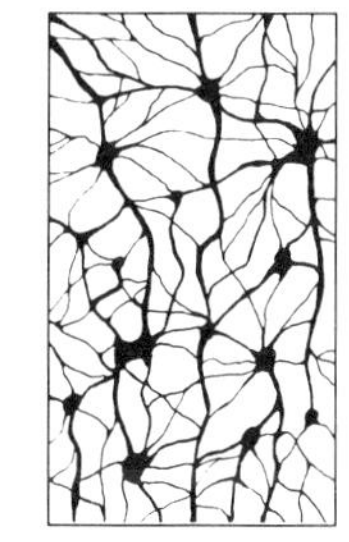

SECTION OF A STIMULATED BRAIN

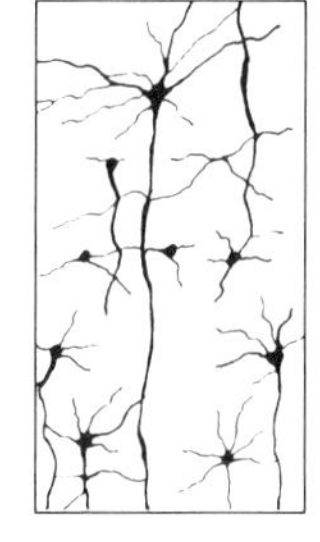

SECTION OF AN UNSTIMULATED BRAIN

The motto is: Use it or lose it! The choice is yours.

The more you use your brain, the better it gets. At any age. The less you use it, the fewer brain cell connections you make, and eventually its capability will decline.

More about your thinking brain

Imagine you are looking down on top of your head and are able to see through your skull to the thinking brain within. What you would see is that the thinking brain (or neo-cortex) consists of two distinct halves. These are the **Cerebral Hemispheres**. The two halves are connected by a rich bundle of nerves.

Ingenious research suggests that each hemisphere, or half of the brain, tends to have its own style of processing information for learning.

Left Brain specialities

Speech
Step-by-Step logic
Numbers

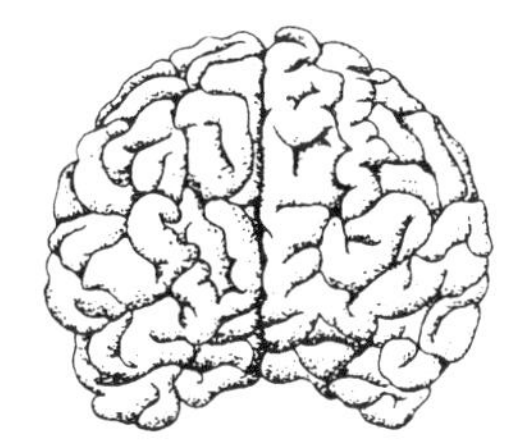

Right Brain specialities

Melody
Patterns
Intuition

It's important not to exaggerate the difference, because our brains are far too complex to be put into neat categories. Nevertheless, there is an important lesson to learn from this research.Some people prefer a slow step-by-step build up of information. We call them the more "linear" type of learner.

Others prefer – indeed, absolutely need – to see the "big picture" of the subject. To have an overview so they can see where it all leads to. (It's difficult to do a jigsaw without the picture on the box in front of us!) We call them the more "global" type of learner.

'The brain may well be like a miracle computer. But it's also the only one that runs on glucose, generates 10 watts of electricity and is created by unskilled labour!"

David Lewis

When we listen to a song, the left brain will basically be attending to the words, the right brain will be attending to the melody. In addition, the emotional centre of your brain, or limbic system, will be engaged. **In other words your whole brain is actively involved.**

Now think how comparatively easy it is to learn the words of a song. You probably know dozens, maybe hundreds of songs – yet you normally make little conscious effort to learn them.

ACTION

Take a few moments to think about what you have just read.

The conditions under which you listen to a song are usually relaxed and stress free. What does this information tell you about the conditions for effective learning?

Does it make sense to combine activities that involve the whole brain as we learn? Combine, for example, pictures and words? Or words and music? Or the overall big picture with detail?

Are you asking questions as you read?

A question you might ask right now is . . . "Am I more of a Linear or Global learner?"

A very simplified way to explain the difference between "linear" and "global" thinking would be to imagine meeting someone you know.

A totally "linear" approach would be to build up the image step-by-step. You would scan the hair, the forehead, then the eyebrows, the eyes, nose, mouth and chin. It is a slow, logical, build up of information in sequence.

Of course we don't do that. We glance at the person and instantly our capacity for global thinking means we see the **pattern.**

The result is we immediately recognise we know the person.

Here's why the distinction between "linear" learners and "global" learners matters. Most traditional educational materials rely too heavily on a linear presentation i.e. a slow, detailed, build up of information. The more "Global" learners get frustrated. They cannot see where it's all leading to. So they get bored and switch off.

The style of teaching that used to characterise our educational system was typically "sit still, face the front, and listen to me".

That style of teaching suits less than half the population.

No wonder so many people feel they could have done better at school than they did. And that feeling still affects their attitude to learning years later.

Most of our learning experiences have tended to be based on the type of instruction that "Linear" learners like.

This is sad for people who like intuitive thinking – school rarely enables them to achieve their full potential. It is also sad for those who rely more on a linear type of thinking – they have not been given the chance to develop more creative and intuitive styles of thinking.

Problem

Absolutely stuck with something new you are learning? Unable to retain it? Unable to maintain interest and concentration while you read.

"In a rapidly changing environment, people will need to move in and out of education all their lives."

Professor Tom Stonier
Bradford University

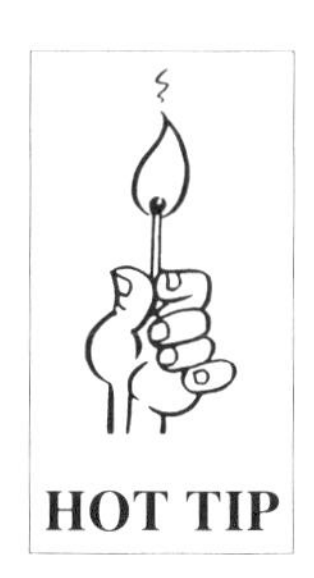
HOT TIP

Look at the way you are approaching it . Can you identify your approach as linear or global?

For example, if you are laboriously working your way through a text book taking careful notes – try something radically different. Try using some visual images – take a range of coloured pens and create a poster that represents what you are trying to learn. You will have changed from a linear approach to a more to a whole brained mode of learning.

Learning challenges aren't confined to work or school!

Today's citizen needs to cope with programmable CD players, programmable washing machines, hi-tech V.C.R.'s, high-tech medicines, and hi-tech home computers. (Coming soon – inter-active TV where you can actually take part in a live show from your armchair). This programme therefore helps with every aspect of your life – work, school and leisure.

What Has All This Brain Stuff Got To Do With Learning?

Simply this. Information entering our brain will travel to the middle brain. The middle brain acts as a sort of central switchboard. If it decides the information is worthwhile, it switches that information up to your "thinking brain".

Now remember that this middle brain is not only a "switchboard", it is also the part of your brain that controls your emotions. So, when the new information is transmitted to you in ways that appeal positively to your emotions, you can learn well and remember well.

When what we are learning includes colour, illustrations, games and sometimes a musical accompaniment, our emotions are engaged positively, and we learn better.

Which teachers do you remember from school? Chances are the ones who are or were enthusiastic. Enthusiasm has emotional appeal.

However, when negative emotions or fear are present, the middle brain may suppress the incoming information.

If you are under stress, information may never even reach your thinking brain. It gets filtered out. That is what happens when your mind goes blank.

STRESSED OR STRETCHED?

There is a difference between stress, which is negative, and the feeling of tension you get before you start something that you know will stretch your ability.

We all feel good when we rise to a challenge. A game with an opponent with whom we need to struggle to win.

Or mastering a hobby or a school subject or a new skill at work.

To be stretched is positive – it makes life fun.

STRESSED **RELAXED**

Stress, however, is not only the worry and concerns that you are conscious of. Very often people with a poor previous experience of learning feel unconsciously threatened by new learning experiences.

It becomes a vicious circle. Because they feel they are poor at learning, they feel threatened. And because they feel under threat their thinking brain receives less information, so they do learn less effectively.

If you feel insecure, less of your brain's potential is available. That is why, when you are worried, you may suddenly come to realise that you had been staring at a page, without taking anything in.

The secret is to get into a calm positive mood, **before** you start learning.

The Good News –You Have Seven Intelligences To Use

We have seen that you have certainly got the brain capacity. With 100 **billion** brain cells, you would have to be downright greedy to want any more!

But how do we actually use our brain to learn? Why do most of us use only a tiny fraction of its potential? And what is intelligence?

Work by Dr. Howard Gardner at Harvard University points to the fact that we have not just "an" intelligence – but seven.

Each intelligence is of **similar** importance in reaching our full human potential.

Let's look at those seven important intelligences. They are common sense. We can recognise them as natural talents, which each of us has to a greater or lesser extent.

The seven intelligences are:

1. **Linguistic Intelligence** – or talent with language

   The ability to write or talk well. Some people just seem to have the "gift of the gab". Or they can write well. Many people like to read good novels, or even write poetry. They have good linguistic intelligence.

2. **Mathematical/Logical** intelligence – or talent with maths, logic and systems.

   The ability to deal well with numbers and to think logically. You probably know people who perhaps do not think of themselves as "intelligent", but who are razor sharp in adding up the odds on a bet, or at marking score at darts!

   Engineers, scientists and accountants would demonstrate this intelligence.

3. **Visual/Spatial Intelligence** – or visual talent.

   The ability to visualise how things will eventually look. To imagine things in your mind's eye.

   Designers, architects and artists would be an example, but **you** use it when you use your sense of direction, navigate or draw well.

4. **Musical Intelligence** or talent with music.

   The ability to create and interpret music. To keep rhythm. Most of us have a good basic musical intelligence and we can all develop it. Think how helpful it is to learn with a jingle or rhyme? (e.g. 30 days hath September.)

5. **Bodily/Physical Intelligence**

   You use this intelligence when you move well, run, dance, build and construct something. All arts and crafts use this intelligence.

   Many people who are physically talented and "good with their hands" do not recognise that they are showing a high form of intelligence. One that is of **equal value** to the other intelligences.

6. **Inter-Personal Intelligence** – or social talent.

   The ability to communicate well and get on with others. Many people have a superb ability to make people feel at ease, to read others' reactions and to be sympathetic to the feelings of others.

   This is a vital human intelligence. This talent is used to the full in being a good parent, a supportive colleague or a good teacher.

7. **Intra-Personal Intelligence** or inner control.

   An ability for quiet, objective, self-analysis. This leads to being able to understand your own behaviour and feelings.

   You use this intelligence to create your own goals and plans, and to study your own successes and mistakes as a guide to future improvement.

It is worth spending a few minutes looking at this list of seven intelligences or talents again. **Be aware that they are of equal value**.

This new way of looking at people's ability has lead Dr. Howard Gardner to propose a new definition of "intelligence". It is "the ability to create useful products and solve everyday problems".

"A uniform way of teaching and testing is patently unsatisfactory when everyone is so different."

Dr Howard Gardner
Frames of mind

Previously, intelligence was defined much more narrowly. It was mostly related to academic performance. Yet academic subjects are largely taught through just **two** intelligences – the linguistic and mathematical/logical intelligences.

Academic success is indeed one way of demonstrating intelligence. In the real world, however, it is **far** from the **only** way.

Using ALL your intelligences

People nowadays are learning maths through songs, chants and jingles. They are learning by physically handling counters, by actually picturing the pattern that numbers make, by working together in pairs, through imagery, through colour charts and diagrams. And they are loving it.

Success in learning is much broader than simple academic success.

Think of people like Richard Branson or Winston Churchill. They weren't particularly successful in formal education – yet Richard Branson is a multi-millionaire and Winston Churchill won the Nobel Prize for literature.

People are learning to write **really** creatively by using Learning Maps. They are making vivid mental pictures before they start writing, they are acting out parts of their story and they are seeing the value of working in pairs.

The point is this. We do indeed need to be fluent with words and good with numbers. But there are **lots** of new, interesting and enjoyable ways to become literate and numerate – when you start to use your own strengths, and your **full** range of intelligences.

It is the unique way in which these intelligences are combined in us that accounts for the fact that we each have our own personal learning style.

How Modern Research Has Changed Six Assumptions About Learning

The **old** Thinking	The **new** thinking	What do **you** think?
1. We are normally discouraged from moving around while we are learning.	Now we know that some people need to get up and move in order to learn. They are the more physical learners.	
2. We are too often given the theory first, but not allowed enough opportunity to try it out through "hands on experience".	Most people learn well when they can act first, then theorise or reflect afterwards. **Learn through experience – and that includes mistakes!**	
3. We are usually told not to talk out loud while we are learning.	Now university researchers have found that talking a problem out loud and summarising what you are learning out loud in your own words is not a sign of madness! It is an important learning skill.	
4. We are normally told not to "cheat" or discuss the subject with other people.	We now know that "co-operative" learning, where learners pair up to teach and test each other, is a huge advantage. When you see how someone else tackles the subject, it not only gives you a new view, it is more enjoyable!	
5. Most subjects are presented bit-by-bit, building up the detail towards a final conclusion.	Many people need the "big picture" first and are often left confused by a "tedious" build up of information. It's difficult to do a jigsaw without seeing the picture on the box. When you get a quick "feel" of the subject first, you can see how it all fits together.	
6. The old assumption was that the trainer or teacher was the instructor. His or her job was to fill the empty heads of the students with knowledge! The teacher took the central, active, role, the students the passive role – waiting to be "filled up".	We now know that learning with understanding is not like that at all. Learning must be an entirely **active** experience. The teacher or trainer can only provide the conditions in which **you** want to learn.	

We have explained how these six old assumptions have now been overturned, because the new way of learning is **very** different. So, however you may have felt about learning in the past, the message is this – **you can choose to change**.

Conclusion

You have **all** the capacity you need to be an excellent learner.

To all intents and purposes the basic capacity of a human brain is limitless. Most people however, use only a fraction of their true potential, for three reasons:

1. They lack self-confidence.

2. They lack an organised approach to learning.

3. They do not know how to learn so that they use their **preferred** learning style and their **full** range of intelligences.

This programme is designed to ensure that you know how to learn in ways that suit **your** unique mix of capabilities.

The programme is also designed so that you have a clear step-by-step plan to work to. That plan is based on the Six Stages of Learning we have already outlined.

Let us now remind ourselves of those six stages in visual form.

Six Stages Of Learning

Get into the right state of mind

Relaxed, Confident and Motivated.

Get the facts to suit yourself

Ensure you have registered the information visually, aurally and physically.

Explore what you are learni
with your . . .

3

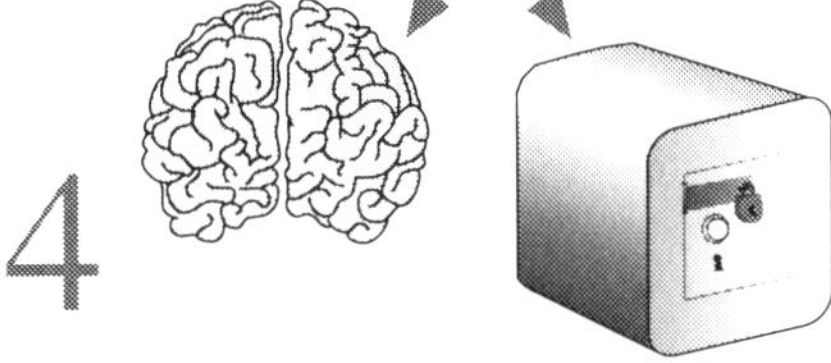

Memorise the key facts

One or two key facts should trigger the rest of what you have learned.

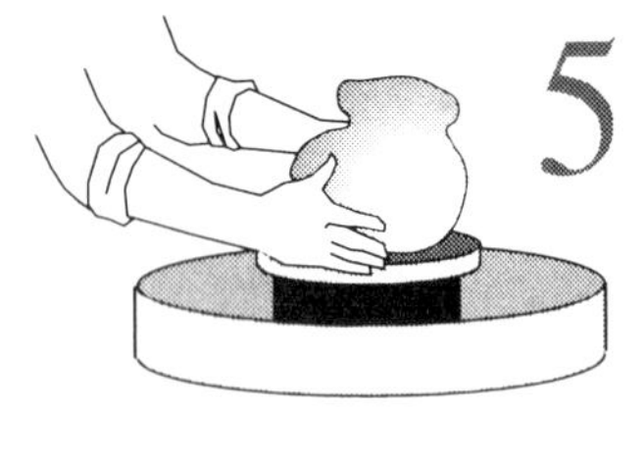

Show you know

Test out whether you really know it, then practise and use it.

Reflect on how you've learned

So you continuously improve the methods you learn with.

Check what you learned so far

1. Why are many people uncomfortable with "academic type" learning, and yet can learn well in "informal" settings?

2. "Adults are just children with big _ _ _ _ _ _." What is the missing word?

3. Is learning with other people distracting or helpful?

4. Why does it help to explain what you have learned to someone else?

5. "How you behave is based on what you _ _ _ _ _." Fill in the missing word and explain what the phrase means.

6. Learning can "go in one ear and out the other", unless you stop and do what?

7. What do you need to do to ensure you really understand a subject?

8. Can you yet name the Six Stages of Learning without looking back at the text?

    1.
    2.
    3.
    4.
    5.
    6.

Answers on Page 214

How we will proceed

Having identified six clear Stages of learning, let's examine these together – stage-by-stage.

Remember to take regular breaks, and use the power tools from the booklet to tackle this more comprehensive manual.

On pages 210/211 there is a complete summary of this whole programme. It allows you to tick off the ideas that you find work best for you. You may like to refer to it as you finish each Stage. It will help you "custom-make" your own plan of action for learning.

A time for reflection

If you are a learner at work:

- The main ideas from this section that I will use in my job or career are:

- Although I originally did well in my studies, I can see that there are ideas here to learn even better in future. They are:

- I didn't achieve everything I could have done at school. But I could start to realise more of my true potential, if I:

- Tthe following ideas will enable me to help the people I am responsible for:

- As a parent, the ideas that can help my children are:

If you are a student:

- The ideas I am going to use to help me learn more effectively are:

- Some of the ideas are worth talking over with my friends. They are:

- I really feel I would like to discuss some of these ideas with my teacher or tutor. They are:

Stage One

Get into the right state of mind for learning

Worth Pondering on!

- Walt Disney was fired by a newspaper editor because he lacked "good creative ideas".
- Einstein could not speak until he was four, and could not read until he was seven.
- Beethoven's music teacher told him he was "hopeless as a composer".
- Paul Gaugin only tried painting because he failed as a stock broker.
- Rodgers and Hammerstein's first collaboration was so disastrous that they didn't work together again for years.
- Writer Marilyn Ferguson puts it so well:

  "Your past is not your potential."

  It's never too late to succeed. High achievers are made – not born.

Introduction

How you feel about learning is extremely important.

If you feel good about your ability to learn, this first section contains many ideas that will reinforce and extend that confidence.

If, like many others, you have lacked confidence as a learner, it's important to know that you are not stuck with those feelings.

Nevertheless, changing your attitude – whilst entirely possible – will require some deliberate effort to put into practice some proven techniques.

A positive attitude to learning flows from:

1. Understanding your feelings, how they are formed and how you can choose to change them.

   Knowing how to take **deliberate** action to create the strongest possible belief in your own ability. Self-belief is the key to success.

2. Being able to set clear goals, because to spend time to learn means choosing from competing possibilities. Your motivation to choose study over a more immediate pleasure, depends largely on how clear your vision of your future success is.

3. Knowing how to allocate your time effectively, because learning involves spending your time which is limited.

4. Being able to relax and calm yourself whenever you need.

Feelings And Self-Belief

Prologue

Imagine you are in the kitchen. You take a fresh lemon from the fruit bowl. It is cool in your hand. The yellow dimpled skin feels smooth and waxy. It comes to a small green conical point at either end. The lemon is firm and quite heavy for its size as you look at it in the palm of your hand.

You raise the lemon to your nose. It gives off such a characteristic, unmistakable citrus smell, doesn't it?

You take a sharp knife and cut the lemon in half. The two halves fall apart, the white pulpy outer skin contrasting with the drops of pale lemon coloured juice that gently ooze out. You raise the lemon towards your mouth. The lemon smell is now slightly stronger.

Now you bite deeply into the lemon and let the juice swirl around your mouth. That sharp sour lemon flavour is unmistakable.

Stop a minute!

Did your mouth water? Almost everyone's does. And yet the extraordinary thing is that if we had simply instructed you to "make your mouth water", you couldn't have done it.

The "imagery" worked because your emotional middle brain does not distinguish between experiences that actually occur out there in the "real" world, and experiences you imagine vividly in your head.

You can use this fact to "programme" your emotional brain to believe very strongly in your success. It is important to do this programming – because it is frightening how quickly and unnecessarily we create self-doubts and self-limits.

How Feelings Are Formed

You have probably heard of Pavlov's dogs. Pavlov was a Russian research psychologist who proved that the mind connects events with feelings and emotions to produce instinctive behaviour.

He would ring a bell every time he fed his dogs. Gradually the dogs came to associate the ringing of the bell with food. So their mouths would water when the bell rang – even when there wasn't any food. It's called a stimulus-response mechanism. The bell was the stimulus. The automatic response was for the dogs to salivate.

The sequence is:

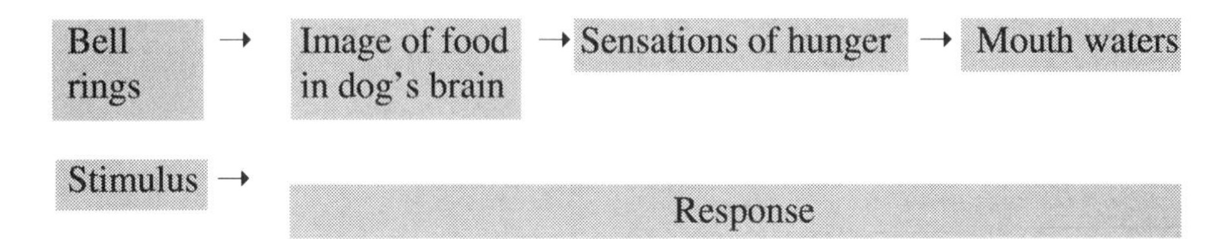

Through repetition a stimulus/response pattern is created which causes chemical changes in the brain. A strong memory trace is formed and a "habit of mind" is created.

In the same way as a past experience can create a physical response, so a past experience can create an **emotional** response.

One or two unsuccessful attempts at mathematics, for example, get changed in our subconscious into a totally different statement – "**I'm** no good at maths".

"I failed this time" becomes, "**I'm** a failure". Yet they are **totally** different statements.

All attitudes are learned attitudes

If 2x – x = 5 What is x?

How do you **feel** when you look at that equation? Lots of people feel tense in their stomach. Possibly a feeling of helplessness or even incompetence.

When you are faced with a learning situation that stimulates an unhelpful response, it's rarely just a feeling that you get. There's normally some words that go with it! They go something like, "Oh no! Not a mathematical problem! I'm going to mess this up".

So when you hear people say "I don't like Maths", or "I don't like being in a

*Because mathematics **is** such a common fear for many people, we have used it as an example.*

*If you are good at mathematics don't be smug – substitute a subject you feel you are **not** good at: Like public speaking, drawing or reading large handbooks like this!*

training room – it reminds me of school", what they are really saying is "I don't like the **feeling** and **thoughts** I get when I'm faced with Maths, or a training day".

*(By the way, **x** = 5)*

These feelings towards mathematics are merely unhelpful responses someone has learned. The problem is that those uncomfortable feelings, and the negative words you say to yourself, create stress. This stress, as we have learned, can block learning, leading to further loss of confidence. So it's important to work deliberately to create a highly positive state of mind!

The key point is this. The response you get from a stimulus, isn't fixed. **You learned it. And if you learned one response – you can choose to learn another.**

Just as people can **un**consciously generalise a single error into a feeling of defeat, so you can **consciously** generalise a single moment of success into a general feeling of confidence. You'll learn how shortly.

Everything is possible

Barbara Meister-Vitale was dismissed as a retarded child. She couldn't read at twelve and was pronounced as "hopelessly dyslexic".

Her grandmother never gave up on her – she encouraged her to use her talent to draw, create mental images, and to play music. Gradually she learned to use more of these visual and rhythmic talents to explore her school work. It helped reduce her reliance on the written word.

Today she is a member of MENSA, and has two degrees including a Masters degree in early learning.

What Success Feels Like

Look at the picture in the margin. It is a picture of someone at a moment of peak experience. A picture, in fact, of an athlete with tunnel vision. He can picture only one thing. Olympic Gold.

It's a state of exaltation, of knowing deep in your mind, deep in your body, that you created a moment of excellence. It's a moment of great clarity, when everything came together in a moment of total **inner** satisfaction. That feeling doesn't have to last long – then it's on to the next point, the next race or the next task. But that moment lives inside you forever.

That sort of moment is, **literally**, a powerful resource to draw upon. A memory that, if played over and over, will trigger the same feeling of powerfulness inside you. Because the memory of the moment and the feeling that goes with it are inseparable. The memory is the stimulus – the feeling is the response.

Replay the memory and you replay the feeling. Replay the feeling and you've created a resourceful state of mind. **A feeling of strength to draw on when you need.**

From the instant he left the starting blocks, Linford Christie ***knew*** *he was going to win the 1992 men's 100 metre Olympic Gold Medal. He had run and re-run the race in his mind over and over. His eyes were wide open with steely concentration on the finishing line. "All I had to do was focus" he said afterwards.*

Any of the eight finalists could have won. But Christie had the mental edge. The vision.

ACTION

Before you go further we would like you to think back to a time when you did something that was exceptional. A time when everything "clicked". It all came together, and you surprised yourself with your own ability.

It could be a sporting moment. It could be a moment when you suddenly solved a problem, saw a solution in a flash of insight. Maybe you got an "A" grade on a paper, or an exam result beyond your expectations.

It could be the exact moment in a negotiation you suddenly **knew** you would succeed – or the look on someone's face when they congratulated you on an achievement. A perfectly executed dance step, or a meal you cooked that was superb.

It could be an experience with your family or a friend. It could be from a situation where you succeeded in a hobby or a leisure activity.

In other words a peak moment. There are some examples of other people's peak moments on the next page. There is also a place to record your own **specific** memory. If you need help remembering, just look at the illustration above. **That is the feeling.** For a moment time stands still, and you have "the force".

You are not stuck with your feelings.
You can choose to change them!

MY SUCCESSFUL LEARNING EXPERIENCES	*Javelin throw.*	Playing and managing my village football team. Winning a league title for the first time in the club's 40 year history.	Passing physics	Using a woodworking machine router. A very dangerous piece of equipment.
WHAT I AM DOING	*Throwing at an open meeting in Derby 3 years ago. Gaining a club and personal best.*	Choosing a team of the right qualities and using them to the full.	Trying to get to the noticeboard with everyone else crowding round the results.	Trying to take in the detail of what's been said.
SOUNDS WHAT I AM HEARING	*The coach saying just relax, you can beat them. ME: It's a bit windy. I know her – she's meant to be good!*	Some people moaning at the start of the season. At the end 90% of the club were congratulating me.	An absolute hubbub - everyone talking and shouting.	Hold the job down. Keep your hands away from the cutter as it can slip if the grain goes in a different direction.
PHYSICAL SENSATIONS WHAT MY BODY FEELS LIKE	*Adrenaline pumping, heart rate fast, legs shaking, but I knew I was going to do well.*	We won the title on the last game. It was a particularly hard game. Afterwards I felt I could run for miles.	My stomach was churning. Then my fist clenching and a huge release of energy.	Very nervous.
SIGHTS WHAT I AM SEEING	*Running down the runway getting ready to launch. Seeing the javelin fly through the air. I knew it was good.*	Presentation night with a big trophy and me standing on stage with my players.	My result. I didn't just pass, I got an 'A'!	How well it goes when you follow the shape and take your time.
THOUGHTS WHAT I AM SAYING TO MYSELF	*I wanted to shout when the distance was announced. Yes, I've done it. I knew I could. I'll do even better next time.*	I've done it. I've shown all the critics who said you couldn't play and manage a team successfully.	"Wow!" I **did** it.	I didn't think I could do this so easily.
EMOTIONS WHAT EMOTIONS I AM FEELING	*I was so happy I just wanted to shout and tell the world.*	Great! Fabulous!	I wanted to hug myself	Very good and happy. Proud.

Now stop and create a vivid memory of your own learning success. Then fill in the blanks below.

Method One – Creating a resourceful state of mind

You can create a confident, positive state of mind – whenever you choose – with this simple sequence.

You have used this "technique" lots of times without realising it. It is the same mental process that associates "our song" with a particular evening, or a perfume with a particular event.

The song or the perfume always "brings back" the same feeling. Now your "cue" word and the successful image, will bring back a confident feeling. You are merely consciously and deliberately using the same mental process for a positive reason.

Step 1 Recall your moment of success.

Step 2 Now intensify that memory. What did you **see** at that moment? What did you **hear**? What did you **feel**? Get as much detail as possible, using all your senses.

Take some time. See it from your eyes, as you did originally. Hear with your ears, feel with your body.

Avoid seeing yourself in the scene from a distance. It is **essential** that you look out at the successful scene with your own eyes – because that recreates the same feeling of competence and strength that you had originally.

You have learned how to recall a powerful state of resourcefulness. All you need now is a way to call that feeling up, whenever you wish.

Step 3 Having recaptured your moment and feeling of peak experience, think of **one** word that sums up the original event. It is your "cue" word.

Step 4 Sit up straight and straighten your body. Pull your shoulders back. Now look up and take a deep breath. This is important, because at moments of peak experience, we automatically breathe deeply. (You probably already feel different!)

Step 5 Clench your fist – which is a natural thing to do when you feel powerful.

Step 6 Now intensify your memory of that original experience. Really **revel** in the powerful feeling.

Step 7 Unclench your fist and open your eyes.

Repeat this sequence of 7 steps, many times over the next two days. The more often you repeat the sequence the stronger the stimulus/response pattern becomes.

Later, you will be able to return to this resourceful state whenever you wish . Just take a deep breath, picture the scene, clench your fist and say your cue word inside your head. **You've deliberately programmed yourself to feel good and feel competent, on command**.

This is a skill that will benefit you for the rest of your life. It's not just a skill for learning – it's a skill for life.

Not completely convinced yet? Well, remember that when you read about the lemon, your conscious, logical mind knew all along that there wasn't really a lemon to make your mouth water. It was all "in the mind".

Yet it succeeded, because your brain and body respond to the images you create in your own mind in exactly the same way as they respond to "real" outside experiences. That's why we respond physically to dreams or to worry.

Method Two – My list of successes

Everybody has achieved success in learning in their life. You have already chosen one success to imagine in the previous exercise. It may not have been in school, or in a conventional learning situation such as a training day at work, but it has happened for us all.

To recognise our own successes is an important first step in building self-confidence. Confidence is built on experience of success

Sometimes you can make important shifts in attitude through quite small changes. You can change the word "impossible" to "I'm possible" with just one small apostrophe (').

Impossible	I'm possible

ACTION

Personal Record of Learning Successes

List as many successes that you have had in learning as you can. Maybe you would like to illustrate them in the margin?

______________________	______________________
______________________	______________________
______________________	______________________

Here are some successes other people have listed. See how they are from all aspects of personal, school and work life.

Notice how you can also change a negative to a positive with just a simple down stroke of the pen:

In a similar way, you can choose to change your feelings and attitudes towards learning. A positive state of mind will immediately make you more able to learn.

- Teaching myself to use a new computer package in a short time.
- Getting an 'O' Level in Geography when nobody thought I would!
- When I was 8 years old and doing the highest jump in the whole class, even though I was the smallest.
- Learning to instruct and deal with people who are older than me.
- Passing my driving test.
- Learning to get my ideas over to other people so they understand them.
- Being a father and learning tolerance!
- Learning to be a better reader.
- Learning to get on well with people.
- Being more willing to be criticised.
- Understanding double entry bookkeeping.

Creating this record provides you with ample evidence that you are justified in seeing yourself as someone who can succeed.

Method Three – Positive Affirmations

Repeating an affirmation for mental strength is like doing push ups for physical strength.

You don't notice the difference immediately, but the results come with practice.

"The more often I have a good attitude – the more often I have a good day."

Bobbi Deporter

We all have an inner voice – the running commentary in our heads that accompanies our actions. Some of us comment out loud as we try new things. This is good if what we're saying is positive, but much less helpful if we are negative about ourselves.

You can increase your chance of success in whatever you tackle, by thinking and saying really positive things about yourself. You can learn to create and use **Affirmations**. Affirmations are positive statements that express what you choose to become. An example is "I am relaxed and successful in training sessions".

The affirmation need not be true for you **yet** – the time to use affirmations is when you are trying to achieve something.

At first, affirmations describe you as you would like to become. You say the affirmation to yourself (or out loud) over and over. You imagine yourself having achieved something you would like to achieve. The affirmation influences your thoughts and behaviour, and gradually becomes more and more true.

We have no problem in understanding how negative comments have a very real effect on people's thoughts and behaviour. If you tell someone that they are stupid or irresponsible, we all know they will come to be negative and act stupidly and irresponsibly. It's negative programming and it works all too well.

All you will be doing with positive affirmations is using the **same** process, but **you** will be doing the programming to achieve a **positive** effect.

A good example of a simple **positive** affirmation is:

"I AM A CONFIDENT LEARNER"

You can see that affirmations don't need to be complicated or lengthy. Short, snappy affirmations can be more easily remembered and used.

Creating an affirmation

Think about one of your goals. A goal you would normally express as "I wish I was . . .". Now start expressing it positively.

1. Change the "I wish" statement to begin "I choose to be".

   I *choose to be* a good manager.

   I *choose to* play the piano.

   I *choose to* present a paper.

2. Change the "I choose to be" statement to begin "I will".

   I *will* be a good manager.

   I *will* be a pianist.

   I *will* be confident enough to present the paper.

3. Change the "I will" statement to begin "I am".

   I *am* a good manager.

   I *am* a good pianist.

   I *am* confident to present the paper.

Marilyn King, the US. Olympic Pentathlete developed this method to help her succeed in her sport. She has since helped many people use such methods to help them achieve their goals in life.

Top class athletes, sportsmen and sportswomen frequently use these techniques to help them towards success.

Affirmations remind us that we have a choice – to work and succeed or settle for less than we could do.

(Adapted from "Dare to Imagine" by Whisler, Marzano and King.)

Why Affirmations are important

Our minds are programmed day in, day out. Often without us realising it.

Here's a real life example.

Success comes in cans – not can'ts.

A little girl came home from school. She had done her first maths test. She hadn't done very well. Her mother, wishing to be supportive said "Never mind, darling, you can't be good at everything. Think how good you are at art."

The limits to learning are largely self-imposed.

Colin Rose

In that statement – however well meaning – was buried a suggestion that there would always be things that were beyond her capabilities. Everyone of us is **very** suggestible. We build up a picture of the world and our abilities – not only by what we do, but what is said to us.

There was nothing to prevent that little girl from becoming highly proficient at maths. But the statement was the beginning of a belief that she "couldn't do maths".

If we believe we're bad at maths, we will do badly at maths. Because the way we behave needs to fit in with our beliefs.

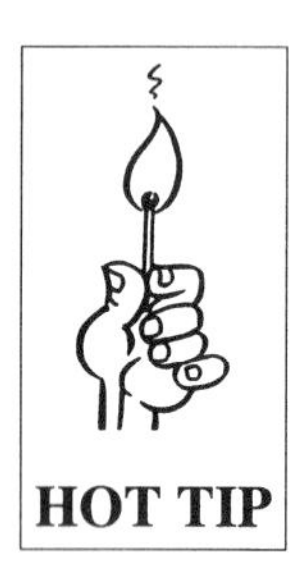

If you are learning in the same place most of the time put up a photo or momento of a past success.

*It's a constant reminder of what success **feels** like and it will help make your mood more positive.*

The sentence you have just read is critical, not just in learning to learn – but in running our whole lives. If you want to change the way you act, you need to change what you **believe**.

If the teaching style for a particular subject at school didn't match your personal learning style, you may have done less well than you could. You could easily have come to conclude that you were a poor learner.

It's necessary to change that belief if your actions are to change – and affirmations are one way. Knowledge about brain capacity and personal learning styles is another. Creating a vision of success is another.

Do you really need to put so much effort into this preliminary stage of learning?

Absolutely. And here's why.

Educational expert Jack Canfield conducted a very imaginative piece of research on school children. He asked a researcher to accompany 100 school children for a whole day, i.e. not just at school. They recorded the number of positive and the number of negative comments made to **each** child over just 24 hours.

The "score" was 72 positive against 684 negative comments!!

Little wonder that although 82% of six year olds are confident of their ability to learn, this drops to 18% of sixteen year olds!

When we have so many negative messages is it any wonder that we need a deliberate bit of re–programming? Affirmations are one good way.

WHY AFFIRMATIONS WORK

Affirmations help create a more positive self-image. A self-image is the picture of yourself you hold in your subconscious.

At the beginning your conscious mind doesn't need to fully believe in them. (Remember how you could make your mouth water by visualising an imaginary lemon?)

But with repetition your subconscious ***does*** *come to believe in your affirmations and looks for ways to make your actions match its beliefs. So gradually a belief in yourself as a confident, effective learner produces the actual result.*

Sounds simple – but our subconscious mind is simple.

ACTION

Try creating your own affirmation using the method developed by Olympic star Marilyn King.

Creating an affirmation

1. Thinking about an ambition, write a statement that begins "I choose to be". . .

____

2. Change the "I choose to be" statement to begin "I will" . . .

____

3. Change the "I will" statement to "I am"

____

____

(Adapted from "Dare to Imagine" by Whisler, Marzano and King.)

This statement is your positive affirmation. It helps you to see yourself succeeding in your ambition.

How to use your Affirmation

The more you repeat your affirmation, the more comfortable you will feel with it. And the closer you will move towards achieving your ambition. Try saying it to yourself frequently and regularly e.g. 10 times in the morning and 10 times at night.

Repeat it to yourself when you are faced with a challenge related to your goal. As you feel more comfortable with it, say it out loud morning and evening. **And imagine the good feelings as your affirmation comes true.**

RELAXATION

You've read why relaxation is so important. And why tension and stress can, literally, make the mind go blank.

That's why we have created the "Shangri–La" exercise on the introductory tape. It's a wonderful way of learning how to relax and reduce tension.

If you play it regularly, you will be able to relax immediately by putting your finger and thumb together and saying "calm", letting the word really sound in you head, feeling your jaw and shoulders relax and go loose.

This is an important exercise before any learning situation. So make a resolution to use it and continue to play the tape regularly. You deserve it.

Modern life is inevitably stressful. Low stress people learn better, live longer and live happier lives.

PROBLEM

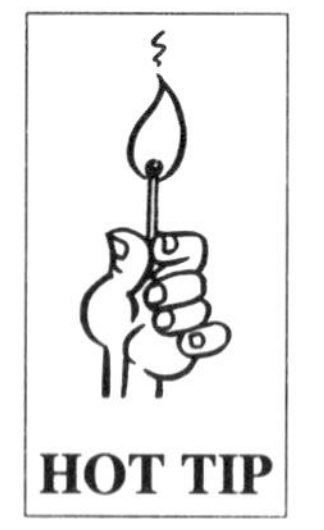

HOT TIP

Want to learn something new but doubt about your ability to tackle it?

Create a positive affirmation about your ability to learn it efficiently. Put it on the wall or by your machine, phone or desk.

Setting Clear Goals

Your Two Minds

We all have a conscious mind. And we all have a subconscious mind. Our conscious mind expresses itself in logical terms. Like "I really should be getting down to learning French tonight" or "I need to study that engineering manual".

Our subconscious mind, however, is much more concerned about how we feel about ourselves. Are we comfortable, happy and safe? Or are we feeling unhappy, pressurised or threatened? Are we confident or apprehensive?

This is where the conflict takes place. To succeed completely you need to make sure that what you consciously **say** you want, and what you really, **sub**consciously **feel** you want, are united.

The image you have of yourself is largely stored in your middle brain. That brain is more likely to respond to an emotional appeal, and to strong images, than to a logical argument. So if you want to change your attitudes, feelings and behaviour, it is important to create a motivating and vivid vision of your future. Such a vision helps programme your subconscious mind to achieve the goals you have set for yourself.

How does this fit into your previous knowledge?

Does this make sense?
Does this challenge or fit in with your experience to date?

Relating and comparing what's new to your existing knowledge and conclusions is a good learning strategy.

Why a vision is so important

To achieve what you want in life, you need to be committed. To have the willpower to succeed you must:

1. Have a **vision** of what you want to achieve.
2. Have a firm **belief** that you can achieve that vision.

People whom we describe as having terrific willpower have a clear idea of what they want, and believe they can do it. This is true of sticking to a fitness training schedule, a strict diet, studying at night school, or getting a qualification.

If you have a vision, you have a purpose and if you have a purpose you create determination and willpower.

"You have to start with the end in mind."

Stephen Covey

Our Definition Of Willpower

A vision is important, because if you don't stand for something – you can fall for anything!

Create with your mind what you cannot presently see with your eye.

WILLPOWER = A CLEAR VISION +
BELIEF IN YOUR ABILITY

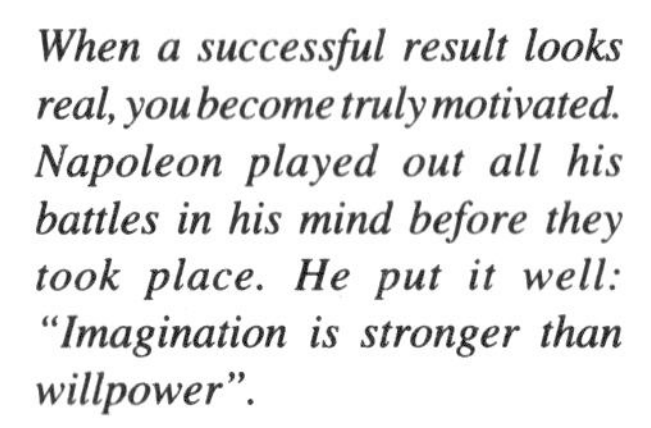

When a successful result looks real, you become truly motivated. Napoleon played out all his battles in his mind before they took place. He put it well: "Imagination is stronger than willpower".

So imagine your success, and you are already half way to achieving it.

This definition of willpower is quite different from most people's definition.

Ask a few people how they define willpower. Chances are they define it as "grim determination", or "gritting your teeth and sticking with it". Ask a few friends and see.

There is an interesting implication in such a definition. It implies a struggle. And the struggle could only be with yourself, right?

Does that sound a healthy state of mind?

It doesn't!

What we do is a result of what we believe and want to do at the **subconscious level**.

It is because you need to have a **crystal clear** vision of what success in learning will bring you, that we have provided "The Motivator" tape. It gives you a simple and relaxing way of creating a powerful and compelling vision of sucess. Take time to play it at the end of this section.

Creating Your Own Vision

To be involved in a learning programme means you have an ambition to "improve". But perhaps it is a pretty vague ambition. The more vague the ambition (vision), the weaker your determination.

So here is a simple question that lets you clarify your ambitions.

Where do I want to be?

1. **In my relationships?**

   What do I want to achieve with the people who matter most to me?

   HINT: If I only had a few months to live, what would I want to do? What would I want to put right? What would I want to say?

2. **In my education or training?**

   What skills do I need – computer/work/languages/numeracy/school qualifications/professional qualifications?

3. **In my job or career?**

   What type of job do I **really** want? What do I feel would make me happy?

4. **In my health?**

   Exercise/sport/nutrition/weight?

5. **In my growth as a well-balanced person?**

   What hobbies, sports, abilities do I want to develop? Do I want to learn to draw, paint, hang-glide, play soccer, golf, write, understand art, music, literature, theatre, films, etc., etc., etc.?

   What do I want to **do**? Where do I want to travel? What would make me proud? Concentrate on what you **feel** is right, not what you think you **should** do!

Take as long as you need to consider the above elements in your life, then continue.

GOAL SETTING IS FUNDAMENTAL

There is no point in being the most efficient oil rig team in history if you are drilling in the wrong place!

"If you really want something badly enough, then usually you can achieve it. It's just a matter of sitting down and setting yourself clearly defined targets."

Duncan Goodhew
Olympic gold medal swimmer

What would you think of an airline pilot who took off without a destination and a basic route map?

Not much!

Your life is a journey. Surely it deserves some clear goals and specific plans?

Turning Your Vision Into Reality

BEWARE OF WISHES!

What we say reveals more than we sometimes think. When someone says "I wish..." what they usually mean is "I'd like to, but it's too much trouble".

When they say "I'll try..." they usually mean "I'm warning you now I may fail". So when they do, they have a let-out clause... "I only said I would try!"

CREATE A CLEAR VISION

Your first step is to create the vision – you need to decide what you want to be.

You need a vision you can see clearly, a goal you can actually see yourself reaching. Ambitions often tend to be expressed in vague wishful words. "I'd love to really make something of myself" . . . "I'd like to get on in my job". "I'd like to do better at mathematics."

"I wish" and "I'll try" have no conviction in them. The only words to use are **"I will . . ."!**

So be honest and **specific** with yourself.

FACT

A recent study was published of the top 2% of "achievers" – people who are acknowledged to be successful in their field.

Whilst they all had different successes they all shared one thing in common. They all had written down their goals in life.

MY VISION OF MYSELF IS

My relationships:

____

____

My education:

____

____

My career:

____

____

My health:

____

____

As a person:

____

____

Now get specific about your vision

A vision describes your overall aims for yourself. Your long-term image. But that needs to be converted into more immediate and **specific** goals. That's the second step.

For example a vision or ambition may be to become confident with all aspects of information technology.

A more immediate and specific goal, however, might be to use a personal computer to manage your finances, records and for word processing.

Here are some examples of how people have turned visions into specific goals.

Their Ambition or Vision	Their Specific Goal
Understand and use computers.	Go on two courses in the next 18 months and actually devise and programme a system that will help some part of my job.
To be able to speak in public.	Present a technical paper to a seminar or conference by December.
To get well qualified.	Pass my H.N.C. and then go on to a degree within 2 years.
To progress in my career.	To be the manager of my section by August.
To pass next year's exams.	To pass all subjects at not less than a 'B' grade.

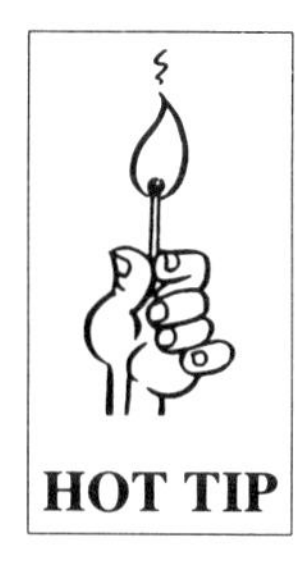

HOT TIP

Create a "symbol of success" to spur you on.

For example, if you were learning French, choose a date when you plan to be good enough to speak comfortably. Then book a weekend in France in advance.

The commitment makes your decision real!

ACTION

Now change your vision into long term goals.

My vision of myself is:	My Specific Goal (s) are:	This is when I'll achieve them:

Why should writing down a goal help you succeed?

Always put a time scale on your goals, otherwise tomorrow never comes!

When you write down a goal you have to think it through more clearly. You can't be vague. The act of putting it on paper makes it more real, more concrete.

If it's a really important goal, put it on a postcard and stick it up where you will see it every day.

*Goals need to be written, seen and **felt** to be motivating.*

ACTION

Sit quietly and **see** yourself as you will be when you've achieved your long term goal.

Where are you? Who else is there? What do they **look** like? Now what do you **hear**? What do people say to you? What do you say to yourself?

Now what do you **feel?**

There's a great sense of uplift in success. Dwell on it. Take a deep breath, look up and smile. Enjoy the feeling.

"Establishing goals is all right so long as you don't let them deprive you of interesting detours!"

Doug Larson

Visualising what you will look like, feel like and talk like when you have achieved your goal, is the **second** step.

Having a clear goal doesn't mean you can't have some fun along the way!

Creating a realistic Action Plan is the **third** step

Now create an Action Plan

You have a motivating vision. You have turned that vision into a more immediate and specific goal. Now you need an Action Plan to achieve those goals. An Action Plan is merely a set of steps you need to take to reach your specific, written, target(s).

To define the steps, you will need to ask yourself a simple question. "What prevents me from getting from where I am now, to where I want to be?"

Do I need:

- Money – how much? Where do I get it?
- Time – how do I free up time?
- Knowledge – where from?
- A skill – how do I acquire it?
- Support – who among my family, friends, colleagues or boss can help?

Below are some examples of how two people began to develop their **ACTION PLANS**.

	Sue	**Alexander**
	Her ambition was to be able to speak in public. She changed this into a clear goal – to present a technical paper at a conference.	He wanted to become a journalist. He formed this into a clear goal – to pass the subjects needed to enter a college of journalism at good enough grades.
Step 1	*Get information from Institute of Mechanical Engineers on how to get a paper accepted.*	*Read books on journalism and good writing. Practice writing. File examples of memorable journalism in a special folder.*
Step 2	*Get support from my manager to allow me to attend some conferences.*	*Get support from my parents, teachers and a cousin who works on a magazine.*
Step 3	*Attend some conferences and observe speaking techniques. (That needs some money for conference fees.) Try speaking at work.*	*Get GCSE and appropriate 'A' levels, including English Literature.*
Step 4	*Prepare a paper in my own time at home.*	*Attend extra evening classes in writing.*
Step 5	*Get time off from work to deliver the paper.*	*Figure out how to get together the college fees.*
Step 6	*Deliver the paper.*	*Attend college and graduate with diploma or degree.*

Your action list

Now convert the goals you have set yourself to an Action Plan.

MY GOALS

Step 1

Step 2

Step 3

Step 4

Step 5

Without clear goals your life can be full of indecision

With a clear vision and goals, priorities become clear. You have a sense of purpose

Now make a "TO DO" list

People who succeed **always** create a list of what they are going to do. They update it each month, each week, and often each day.

The list they make is simple and it is in priority order. This helps them sort out the important from the merely urgent. The important contributes to their Action Plan, the urgent usually doesn't.

A list achieves two things. It concentrates your mind on what needs to be done in order to achieve your plans and therefore your goals. And it gives you a sense of satisfaction when you tick off a task that has been achieved. Sensing progress is an important part of motivation.

You should carry your "To do list" with you and grade it into A's B's and C's.

A's are **must** do's.

B's are **should** do's.

C's are **nice** to do's.

Don't be seduced into doing C's first because they are easier!

And make sure that having some fun is on your A list.

ACTION

Now create a "to do list" that ensures you are working on your action plan today!

IT'S OK TO FEEL CHALLENGED

The only person who really likes change is a wet baby!

If you feel that this programme challenges you to make an effort, that's a sign you are being stretched. And we get the most satisfaction from meeting a stretching challenge.

There's a big difference between feeling tense and threatened by past events – and feeling stretched by a current challenge.

Few pleasures are more intense than ticking off things on your list when you have done them!

Goals can be short term, medium and long term.

Short term might be within a month.

Medium term might be within a year.

Long term might be within 3 years.

Planning Your Time

Not for nothing do we talk about prison as "doing time". When you deprive someone of their right to allocate their time, you are imprisoning them.

Your life is the passing of time. So the words "time" and "life" are, in a sense, interchangeable. To waste time is to waste your life. To use time well is to use your life well.

You and I share one resource in common with the richest, wisest and most powerful men and women in the world.

Take charge of your time and you take charge of your life.

We all have 1,440 minutes in our day.

Time may be democratic, but it is also special and unstoppable. You can't buy it, store it, make it – or change it.

But you can learn to use it better. A video cassette recorder doesn't change time, but it lets you manipulate the time you have to your advantage.

We should pay more attention to phrases like "I will invest time and energy in this". It implies – accurately – that time and energy are more scarce as resources than money. Indeed, you can acquire money with time and energy, but you cannot acquire time and energy with money!

"Every day is a new life to a wise man!"

Bertrand Russell

Yet we think more about how to best use our money – which is renewable – than about how to use our time – which is irreplaceable.

Time then is one of your most valuable – if strictly limited – assets. Whilst you can never physically create time, you can waste it or lose it.

If you learn to allocate your time . . .

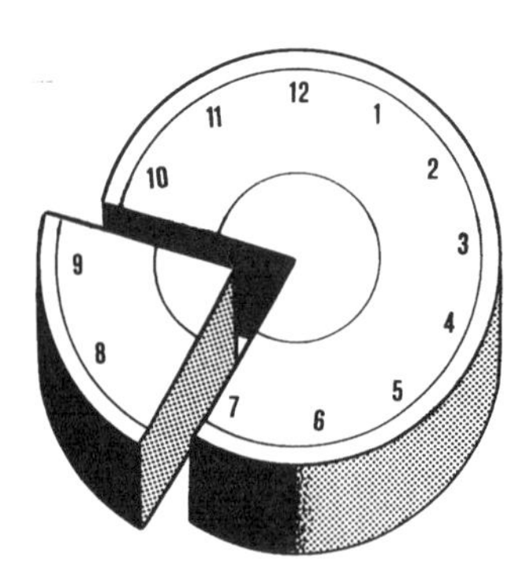

. . . you control your life

Controlling time

You can only control your time if you plan it. That is why this section is not theoretical, it is essential. To plan your time you must know what you want to do with it. So time planning is bound up with goal setting.

The time you take to plan your time is an initial investment that frees up much more time later. It can feel a little artificial or strange initially – but it soon becomes a habit.

To control your time means recognising it is a limited resource. You can't do everything and learning does require you to allocate time. Some things are more important than others, and must be treated as such.

We do the same when we budget our available money. It does not sound strange to say, "I'd like to visit Italy – but I can't afford it". In the same way, we need to be able to say "No" to expenditures of time that don't meet our goals or priorities.

Time is . . .
too fast for those who fear,
too slow for those who wait,
too long for those who grieve,
too short for those who rejoice,
but for those who love,
time is eternity.

Sign in a primary school class in Brunei.

Is it important, or merely urgent?

At first sight this looks like a silly question. Yet it is fundamental to your success that you can distinguish between the two. Can you see the difference between something that is important, and something that is "merely" urgent?

Write down two things below that are urgent, but not important. Then two that are important, but not urgent.

IMPORTANT	URGENT

"The purpose of life is a life of purpose."

Robert Burns

Let us give you some suggestions of our own:

Important but not urgent	Urgent but not important
• Thinking of, and doing something **specific** each week for the people you love. • Taking 30 minutes physical exercise three times a week. • Giving a period of complete attention to your parents and/or partner and/or children. • Deciding what you want to achieve in life. • Defining your priorities for this month and this week. • Having some fun each day. • Actually **doing** the exercises in this course!	• Answering the telephone, to find it is a time-share salesman! • Unexpected visitors. • Being interrupted during a study period by someone who has lost their own concentration and has dropped in for a chat.

Do you notice the underlying difference between what is important and what is merely immediate or urgent?

You decide what is important. **Other** people decide what is urgent.

Of course there are times when something is both urgent **and** important. An accident, for example. But generally speaking the most important things in life are **seemingly** the easiest to postpone.

Look back again at the "Important but not urgent" list. Every one of those items will develop into a crisis if you postpone them long enough.

I say "seemingly" because if you keep postponing the important things of life, you eventually run out of time. Then there is a crisis. A crisis makes important things urgent. But sadly it is often then too late.

You can decide to start an exercise programme tomorrow. As we know, however, tomorrow never comes. One day, (it may be a long time ahead for you), you wake up and your health is gone.

You can put off deciding what your goals in life will be. Except that, one day, you realise that you never got the qualifications for the job that you really wanted.

It is a true tragedy when partners, parents and children realise they "never got round" to telling each other how they felt. To spending the time to really understand each other.

You cannot decide how to allocate your time, until you know what is important.

But how can you know what is important? Define your priorities!

And how can you define your priorities? Decide your goals in life!

So the answer to managing your limited time is:

1. Decide what your goals are.
2. Create an Action Plan to achieve them.
3. Make a regular "to do" list, that sets out your priorities.

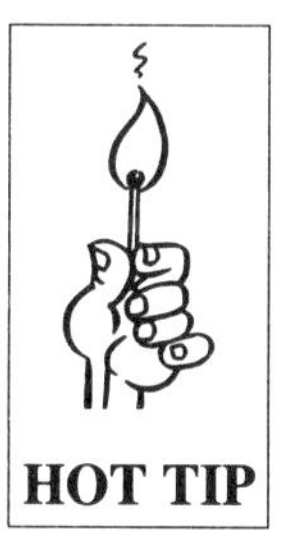

As always . . .

IF IT'S TO BE – IT'S UP TO ME

Twenty years from now you will be more disappointed by what you didn't do, than by what you did do!

So pull up the safety anchor and explore the world about you to the full.

Why Learning Needs Courage

Willing to learn
means
Willing to change

and

Willing to change
means
Willing to take risks

and

Willing to take risks
means
Willing to fail sometimes

and

Willing to fail
means
Willing to analyse
what went wrong – and put it right.

The fruit of the tree is out on a limb!

All change involves risk.

"A funny thing about life. If you refuse to accept anything but the best, you very often get it!"

Somerset Maughan

Why all this planning is worth it!

A vision gives meaning and purpose to your actions. It is the picture on the jigsaw box of life!

We can hear you now! What a lot of effort! What a lot of paperwork! What a lot of theoretical messing about!

Here's the reason why all the planning is worth it.

When you have a vision, a goal, a plan and a "to do" list, your life has a greater sense of direction. If you invest time in actually thinking over the issues that we have reviewed in the last few pages, you will undoubtedly have a greater sense of purpose.

"I can't change the direction of the wind, but I can adjust my sails to always reach my destination."

Jimmy Dean

The goals, of course, will not stay fixed. You will change and modify them along the way, but any change will be **deliberate** and made by **you.** It won't be part of a general drift.

If your life is worth living, it's worth planning. We use phrases like "drifter" and "aimless" for someone who doesn't have goals.

Here are three final thoughts to get the most out of your time.

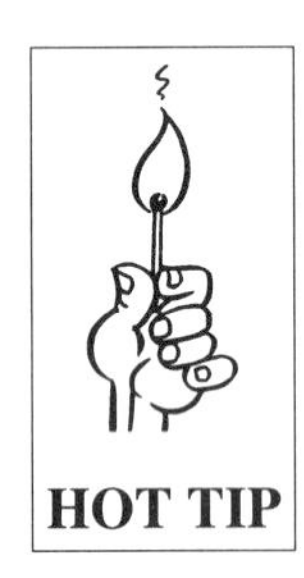

1. Use "down time"

Fifteen minutes a day adds up to over 90 hours in the course of a year. In 15 minutes of waiting for a bus or a train, you could easily learn 10 words of a foreign language – if you wrote them out on flash cards. That's over 3,000 words learned in the course of a year.

What can you learn in your "down time"?

2. Set your own deadlines

Luck is what results when careful planning meets opportunity.

Have you noticed how people manage to accomplish even large tasks when they are up against a deadline. They say proudly, "I did it in the end".

They did – but they were being passive, not active. If they did it in the end, they could equally well have done it at the beginning! The person in control sets her own deadlines.

3. Share your goals

A goal shared with someone else is a more powerful motivator than one you keep to yourself!

When you discuss your goals with someone else, you automatically increase your motivation. It's now a "public" commitment, and you do not want to let yourself down.

Keeping Your Cool

You're confident, you believe in your ability to learn. You have a vision, clear goals and an Action Plan. You have planned your time and are regularly updating your "To Do List".

In real life there are still moments when stress and worry threaten that resourceful state of mind! Here is some advice to deal with tension and stress.

"Whether you think you can – or whether you think you can't – you are probably right!"

Henry Ford

Dealing with the little voice inside

We have seen that we all have a little voice inside our heads that talks to us. Sometimes it is enthusiastic and urging you on. "You can do it". "Great job".

Yet other times it talks to you about worries and concerns, almost without you hearing it.

Now here is a simple but important fact. You cannot listen to two conversations at once!

If someone is talking to you, or teaching you, that's **one** conversation. If there is another conversation in your head at the same time – if that little voice is talking about your worries or concerns – you literally don't hear the teacher or trainer. So you don't learn.

To concentrate you need to "let go" of your worries and silence that inner voice, so that you can concentrate on the trainer, the teacher, or the book.

An effective way is to sit quietly and focus on what that little voice is currently saying. Then imagine that any worries or concerns are balloons. Let them go and see them drift away upwards. Then bring yourself back to the present, ready to concentrate and learn.

Why not sit quiet RIGHT NOW. Focus on what is going on in your head. Can you hear that little voice? Even the one that says, "I can't hear a little voice". Yes that's the one we mean!

The two monks

Learning to let go of intrusive thoughts is essential to mental health and concentration. There is a famous Zen story that says it all.

Two monks were walking in the early morning. They approached a river which had been swollen by the melting snows into a torrent. The torrent was sweeping right over a small wooden footbridge.

A frightened young woman stood by the near bank. Sighting the two monks, she pleaded tearfully with them to take her across.

Without saying a word, the first monk took her into his arms and held her high as he waded across the footbridge and set her down on the far bank.

The two monks continued their journey in silence until sunset, when their vows of silence permitted them to speak.

The second monk turned on his brother and asked angrily, "How could you have picked up that woman? You know that our vows prevent us from even thinking about women – let alone touching one. You have disgraced our whole order!"

"My brother", replied the first monk, "I put that woman down early this morning. It is you who have been carrying her around all day!"

The Mind-Body Connection

Your physical well-being affects your brain work. Here are two suggestions that will help your ability to learn.

Maximise oxygen

The brain only weighs three pounds, which is about 2% of your body weight. Yet it consumes 20% of your oxygen intake.

So before each learning session, (and throughout the day as needed), close your eyes and breath deeply for just a minute or two.

Sit with your back well into the chair, spine straight. Let your jaw fall loose. Imagine there is a balloon in your stomach. As you breathe in, push your lower stomach out to its fullest limit. Then continue to take in air as your chest rises and expands. Keep breathing in until your chest is fully expanded, and your stomach is now sucked in.

Pause while you hold your stomach in for a moment. Then let the air out with a sigh. Continue this pattern for 5-10 breaths. After you have done this deep breathing, deliberately stiffen and straighten your back, and roll your eyes upwards towards the ceiling.

You will not only feel relaxed – you will feel strengthened and may well want to smile. The word "inspired" comes from the Latin word meaning "to breath in".

Neck Exercises

The connection between body and head is the neck. The human neck was originally evolved to look out for danger – not to spend hours pouring over books! Consequently, tension usually shows up in stiff shoulders and a stiff neck as blood supply is restricted – often by a poor, slumped posture.

A relaxing and energising exercise is to:

- Drop your head and chin forward onto your chest.
- Roll your head sideways to the left.
- Now slowly roll it over to your right shoulder.
- Repeat five times each side.

The exercise clears the tension away from your neck and shoulders.

*Deep breathing, neck exercises and an upright straight spine all allow blood, oxygen and **energy** to pass freely between body and brain.*

Calm focus

Watch a quiz show contestant under pressure. Stress blocks memory and inhibits learning.

So to learn well, you should first relax.

You can learn to relax, **and yet be very alert**, by using a powerful technique called "guided imagery". To do this you'll be using Side Two of the Motivator tape. You'll sit quietly, relax and listen to the speaker. Using his guidance, you will form clear pictures in your own mind of a very beautiful, very peaceful, very relaxing place. A place you would love to be. Sunny, warm and calm, a sub-tropical paradise. Which is why we call it your personal Shangri-La.

Then, as you are listening to the tape, and feeling very relaxed and very peaceful, the voice will suggest that you press your finger and thumb together. That action begins to link together the feeling of calm relaxation and the act of pressing your finger and thumb together. It is the start of a deliberate, self-made, stimulus/response pattern.

By repeating the tape, and practising the skill in spare moments, you will in future be able to create a feeling of calm focus, **at will**. Your brain will have associated the act of pressing your finger and thumb together with a feeling of relaxed calm.

You will have trained yourself to be able to relax on demand, and that is a very valuable skill.

Tension burns energy and distracts attention

You often feel tension where the head joins the body – in the neck and shoulders. That is especially true for students and people who work with their heads. We evolved our neck for the frequent movements involved in hunting and gathering – not for holding it still over books and papers. You also experience tension by tightening your jaws together or grinding your teeth.

Why do we experience such tension? Through fear and pressure of work. Insecurity, work load or fear of failure make us tense up at imaginary scenarios. The result is to cause unnecessary energy to be burned, and attention to be diverted.

The study benefits of Calm Focus are obvious. If you clear away distracting tension, you are left with the ability to direct your energy more fully. And directed energy is simply a definition of concentration.

Use this four step sequence to achieve calm focus

1. Pay attention to that internal voice. The one that may be making all the negative, stress producing comments like – "Oh no, not maths! I can't do that!" Make sure you **hear** this type of "subconscious sabotage". Don't let your subconscious talk behind your back! **You can't change what you're not aware of**.

2. Physically shift your position. If you're sitting, stand. If you are standing, move. Your mind and body are so closely linked together, that by changing position you can often start to shift your thoughts towards new possibilities.

   A new perspective means looking at something from a different direction. You can start to achieve a new direction by moving.

3. Once you've brought any concerns into the open, and moved to a new position, then enter a calm state by **taking a deep breath,** and by pressing your finger and thumb together. Visualise your special secure place, your Shangri-La.

4. Replace any negative thoughts with the positive statements you will have learned on the tape or with your own affirmation.

   That four step sequence may take a maximum of one or two minutes. In that short time, however, you can create an important component of successful learning. A state of calm focus.

Other ways you can relax

1. Tense your body, then relax your muscles several times. Tensing first makes you very aware of the presence of tension in your body, and of the contrasting sensation of relaxation.

2. Listen to relaxing music of your own choice, with your eyes closed.

3. Count backwards from 10. After each number exhale and say to yourself. "I am even more relaxed now".

4. For some people, tension is dispelled by physical exercise such as a walk, swim or a game.

The important point about relaxation is to use what works for you.

Catch yourself doing it right!

This simple but effective idea is adapted from a very good book entitled *"The One Minute Teacher"* by Spencer Johnson.

The idea is **deliberately** to look for occasions when you did something right or learned something well.

Having "caught yourself doing it right", you simply praise yourself for it. Something straightforward will do, like "Helen, that was really good, well done."

The basis for this deceptively simple idea is very sound. If you want to change someone's behaviour, you do so by rewarding them when they get it right – not by punishing them when they get it wrong!

Unfortunately, there are not so many times when someone else notices your little successes – or even big ones! Hence the value of noticing each and every little one of your own successes. And praising yourself.

Big changes rarely come in one leap. They are almost always made up of lots of small steps forward. This idea of "catching yourself doing something right", recognises this important truth.

Give yourself a "pat on the back" for each learning success, and every time you use what you have learned from Accelerate Your Learning.

Talk positively to yourself.

"I got on really well there."

"I made the effort and I succeeded."

"I'll use that method again."

"That was great."

Make sure that you really pay attention to the good ***feelings*** *you experience from each mini-success.*

When can you catch yourself doing it right? Now would be a good time. After all you are making the effort to read this Handbook!

Another excellent idea is to keep a record of your successes in your "Learning Log". See page 193.

Notice each time you do something right – and comment on it to yourself.

Problem

Sometimes find yourself tempted to give up? Find it difficult to keep working on something you are trying to learn once the initial enthusiasm has gone?

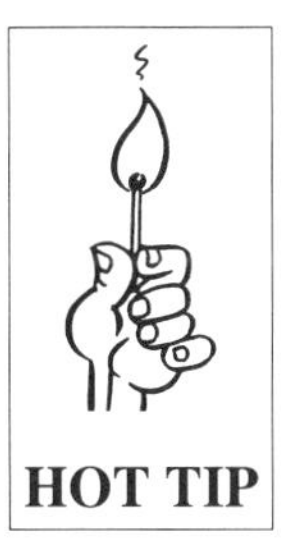

Plan in a reward for yourself each time you achieve a short-term goal. Congratulate yourself on your staying power and take time out to enjoy whatever you have promised yourself.

And be sure to work on creating a really powerful image of your success.

Decide on some suitable rewards right now.

1.

2.

3.

Your reward list might include reading a favourite magazine, a celebration meal, a trip to the movies, a favourite piece of music.

Success rarely comes in one big leap. You can only climb a mountain step-by-step.

If every time you progress a step forward you remember to notice it, then you will come to associate learning with feeling good. That's all part of motivation!

Super self-motivation!

If you can motivate yourself to do one thing – get out of bed for example – you can almost certainly use the **same** sequence of activities to motivate yourself to do anything else. The same tone of voice, the same type of words, the same type of mental picture in your mind.

Think about the "strategies" you currently use to motivate yourself – to make an extra effort to win a game for example. Do you talk to yourself? If so, in what tone of voice? How loud? Is it enthusiastic? Or threatening?

Do you imagine the end result? Do you picture how wonderful it will be to have achieved your objective? Or do you picture the dire consequences if you don't?

Here is a skill that can aid you throughout your life. If you want to do something, ask yourself "Have I ever done something like this before, in any other situation? How did I do it then?"

Then apply the **same** sequence of activities to the new situation.

We all walk around with programmes in our heads. Most of the time these programmes are unconscious. With some deliberate effort you can make the same process conscious, and therefore available for your use.

Your environment counts

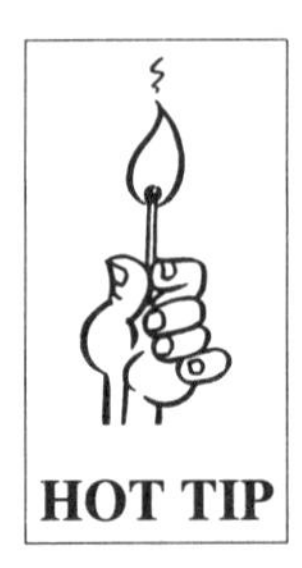

We have made a number of suggestions of how to make the environment in which you learn conducive to success.

Experiment with different lighting and even background music. The total effect has a real impact on how well you learn.

SUBCONSCIOUS PROMPTS

We pick up a lot of our knowledge from "cues" that we are scarcely aware of. But they influence our state of mind all the same.

Try putting up a really beautiful poster or picture where you learn or study.

Or some quotations that make you feel good.

There are lots of quotations scattered through this Handbook.

The overall effect is designed to lift your spirits and amuse you. We hope they are working! Use any that take your fancy to make your place of learning more attractive.

The last word on state of mind!

Studies done by Dr. Janice and Ronald Glaser at Ohio State Medical School prove how important it is to be able to control your state of mind. They showed that stress reduces the production of interferon, a substance that's necessary for the efficient working of the immune system. Stress, therefore, weakens your body's resistance to disease.

In addition, the hormones most associated with anxiety, (cortisol and adrenalin), have a depressing effect on the immune system. Small wonder then that colds and other more serious illnesses increase when people are stressed.

All this underlines the importance of the power you now have to create a resourceful and relaxed state of mind. **The power puts you in control**. And the feeling that you are in control of your life is a vital element in maintaining good health.

Dr. George Vaillant showed in his book *"Adaptation to Life"* that mental health is the most important predictor of physical health.

When you see life's stresses as challenges and meet them with confidence, and when you have the ability to create a Calm Focus whenever you want to – **you** are in control.

Remember

Willpower

=

Vision

\+

Belief in your ability

Summary

The amount of time and space we have devoted to State of Mind indicates how important the subject of feelings actually is.

You have been introduced to several practical and proven ways to create a confident, yet relaxed attitude towards learning.

We call this a "resourceful" state of mind, because your attitudes and feelings become a resource, a strength to draw upon. That strength replaces the apprehension that exists in so many people's minds.

In other words you now have useful, positive, methods for getting ready to learn.

As you have been working through this section, you will have begun to see the ideas that are the most useful for you. Transfer these reactions and ideas to the following summary sheet to give you a quick personalised reference on "getting ready to learn".

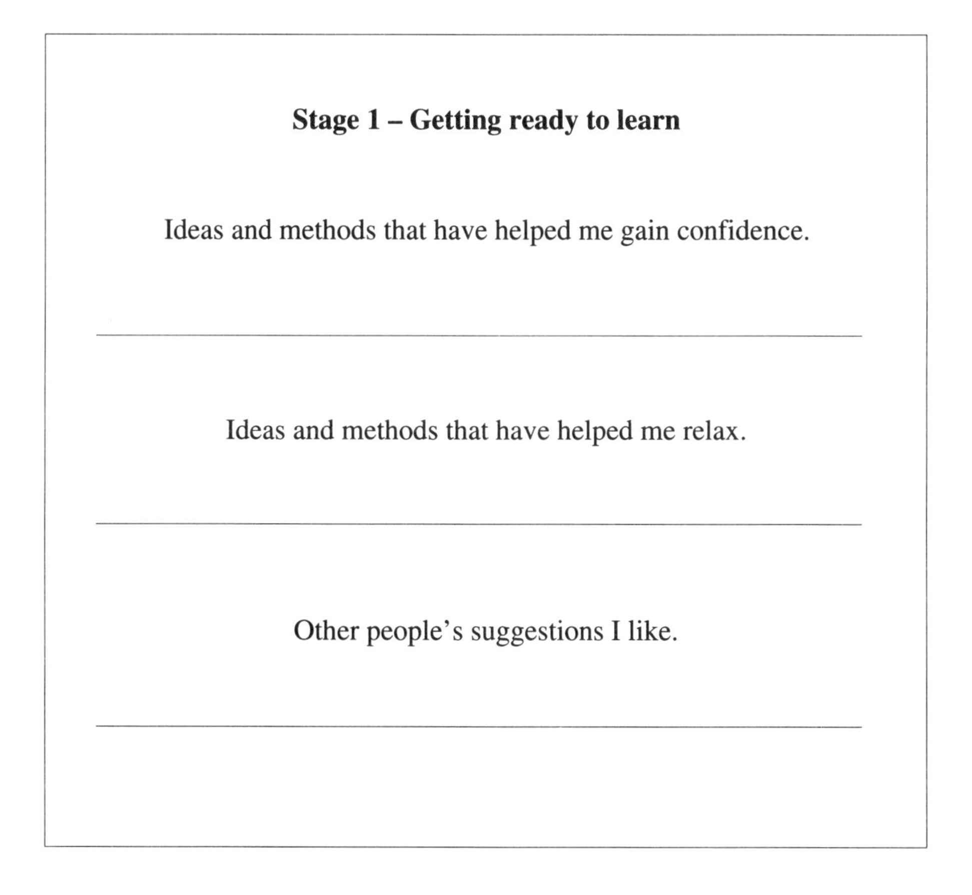

Stage 1 – Getting ready to learn

Ideas and methods that have helped me gain confidence.

Ideas and methods that have helped me relax.

Other people's suggestions I like.

Check what you have learned about Stage One

1. What is the main difference between something that is important and something that is urgent?

2. What three actions let you manage your time efficiently?

3. What is the difference between a vision and a goal or target?

4. What is our definition of willpower?

5. Why is it worthwhile to make detailed written plans?

6. "The limits of learning are . . ." Fill in the missing words.

7. What is an affirmation?

8. Why do we need affirmations?

9. If you want to help change someone's behaviour, (including your own), which will work best? Reward or punishment?

10. Why is it important to relax to create the right state of mind for learning?

Answers on page 214

ACTION

One of the main tools for learning is to keep creating your own questions that need answering.

Are you doing this as you read through this Handbook?

For example, you might have asked yourself

1. **Why** is it important to get into the right state of mind?
2. **Which** methods would work best for me?
3. Should I devote some time to it each time I learn?
4. Should I learn more about relaxation?
5. How often should I review my goals?

Your questions may be entirely different. The important point is to be asking questions.

A Learning Map Of Stage One

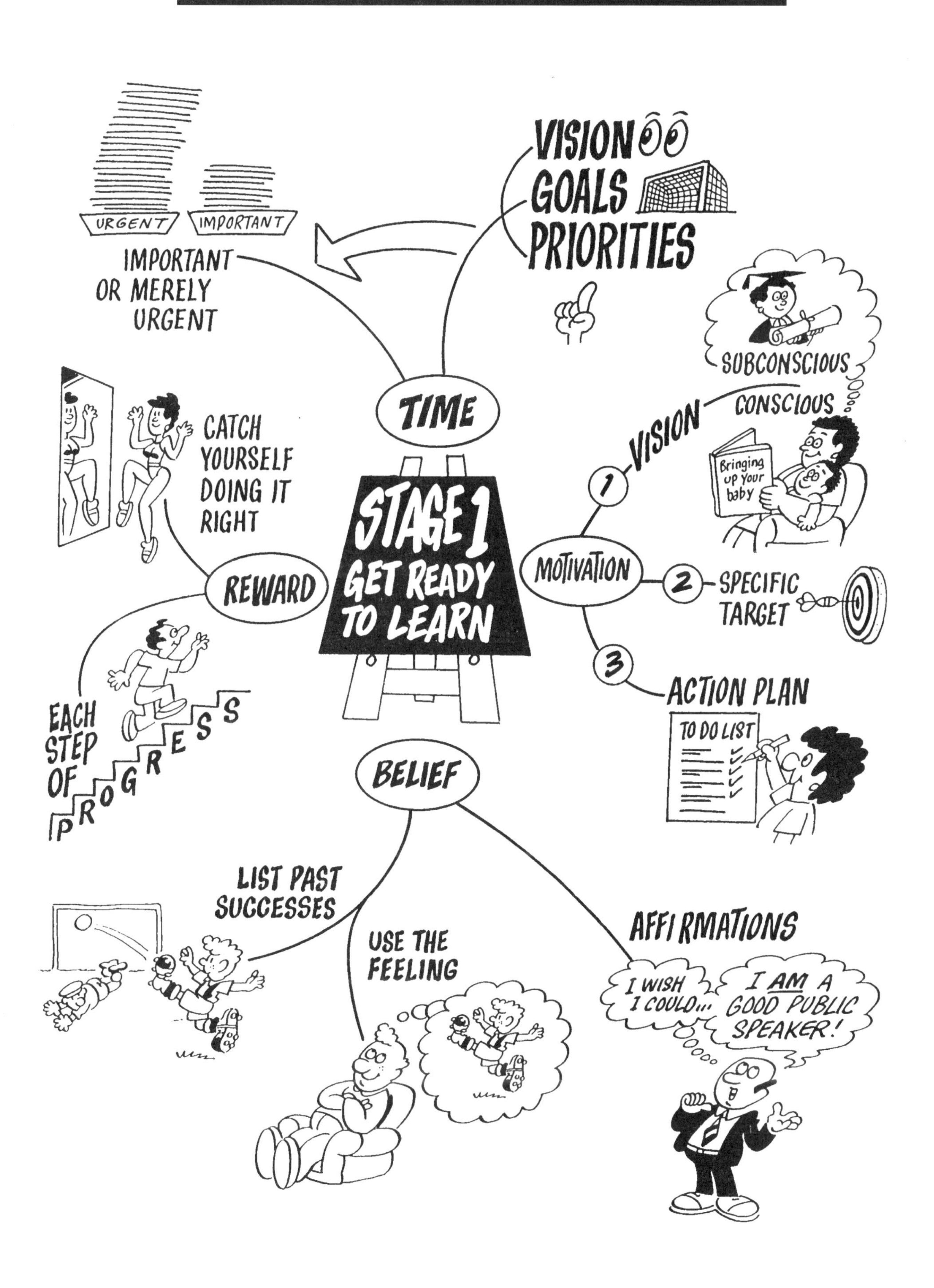

A time for reflection

If you are a learner at work:

- The main ideas from this section that I will use in my job or career are:

- Although I originally did well in my studies, I can see that there are ideas here to learn even better in future. They are:

- I didn't achieve everything I could have done at school. But I could start to realise more of my true potential, if I:

- The following ideas will enable me to help the people I am responsible for:

- As a parent, the ideas that can help my children are:

If you are a student:

- The ideas I am going to use to help me learn more effectively are:

- Some of the ideas are worth talking over with my friends. They are:

- I really feel I would like to discuss some of these ideas with my teacher or tutor. They are:

Stage Two

Get the facts to suit yourself

Use The Tools Immediately

Accelerate Your Learning is a "tool kit" of proven methods that help you learn well. From here on we will either be reminding you to use the tools you know about, or be learning new ones.

You will therefore use the skills of learning – to learn the skills of learning!

TOOLS EXTEND YOUR NATURAL POWER

A lever magnifies the power of your arms. A screwdriver increases the power of your hands. A torch amplifies the power of your eyes in the dark.

These tools of learning extend the natural power of your brain.

REMEMBER

Some of these tools or skills will suit you very well, others will suit you less well. Some will suit some learning situations better than others. Try them out so you can have them **all** in **your learning tool kit**. You can then decide which you want to use and when.

If tools aren't used they go rusty! Keep them polished and sharp.

Look for these symbols

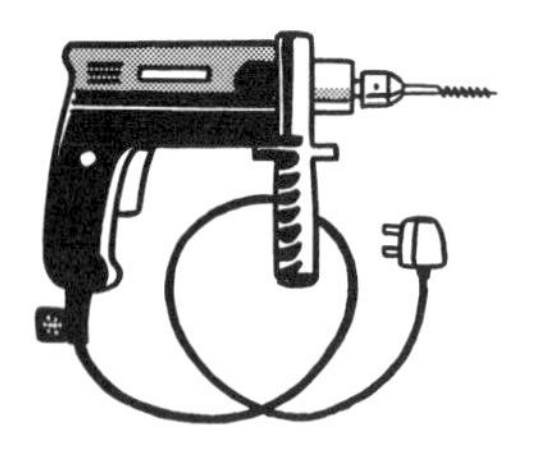

This is a Power Tool
You'll want to use it
all the time.

This is an optional tool.
You'll want to use it if it
suits your learning style,
at the moment.

Get The Big Picture First

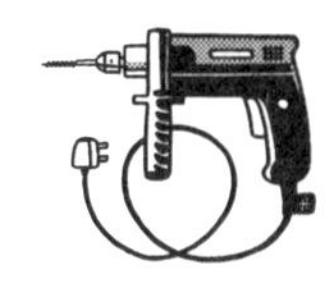

Like most text books this manual has a contents page, sub-headings, illustrations and diagrams.

They are all useful when you are trying to build up an initial impression of the subject. So start with a short "Scan-read" of any new book.

If you are learning from a teacher, a training session or a demonstration, you can get an overview from the trainer or teacher.

Ask for a general outline before the instructor launches into the session. A useful question to ask is "What do you want me to know or be able to do after the session?". What are his objectives for you?

If you are learning from a lecture or film, handouts or programme notes could help. Fast forwarding through a training video gets you an overview.

Scan read a book or chapter first. It gives you the feel of the subject.

You are looking for clues.

PROBLEM

Imagine you are given a manual for a new piece of machinery, a new text-book at school, or a new training manual at work, and are asked to read it.

Feeling you just can't face it? Feeling a bit daunted, and reluctant to get started?

Start by "getting the big picture". And then find something that interests you, and begin with that. You don't always need to begin at the beginning.

BUT DON'T JUMP TO CONCLUSIONS!

Getting an overall picture – or feel – of the subject is important. But remember you haven't got the detail yet.

So don't jump to firm conclusions until you have explored the subject properly.

Many people's main form of exercise is jumping to conclusions!

Remember you have only seen the wood – now you need to examine the trees.

And keep looking ahead!

Looking ahead to see what's coming up next, is not something to do just once.

It's much easier to understand things when you can see where they are leading. So **keep** looking ahead, and continue to build the big picture of what you are learning.

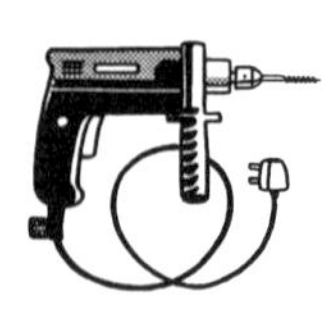

Sketch Out What You Already Know

Jotting down what you already know gives you a clearer picture of your start point. It builds confidence, and it helps define what you don't know!

What do you predict?

HOT TIP

A good way to stay focused on the subject is to stop every now and then and predict what the author, trainer or teacher is going to say or argue.

A good time to start is just after you have decided what you already know about the subject.

So why not spend a minute considering or jotting down the headings of what you know already about *Accelerate Your Learning* and what you realise needs more of your attention.

Because you have "Scan-read" ahead, you will be able to do this.

If you are learning from a lecture or practical training session you should make your notes in the five minutes before it starts.

I already know about . . .	These are areas I need to find more about . . .

A preliminary Learning Map of the subject would be a good way to sketch what you already know.

Then, as you explore the subject in more depth, you can keep adding to your learning map. The map grows as your knowledge grows. The video demonstrates this well.

Break It Down Into Small Steps

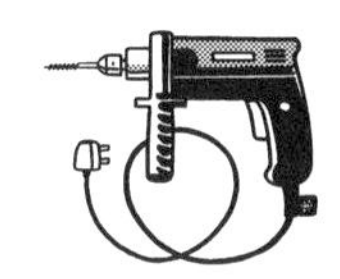

The Chinese philosopher Lao Tzu once said "A journey of a thousand miles starts with a single step."

It's true. However daunting a task may appear, you can crack it with a simple step-by-step plan. That's why we have already included the section on time and planning.

Progress is rarely doing one thing 100% better. It's doing twenty things each 5% better.

This Action Handbook, for example, could be read 7 pages at a time. It would still only take a month.

As a child you learned to talk. Then you learned to read familiar words and phrases. Then sentences. All bit by bit, step by step in manageable chunks.

One researcher has calculated that a child of six has learned more facts about her world than the number of facts needed to acquire a medical degree! It's probably true. She did it, and you did it, piece by piece.

The important point is that when you are learning something challenging – like using a computer for example – you **don't** automatically have to start at the beginning. Roam around the subject and get started on something that engages your interest.

Einstein had to start somewhere!

As has often been pointed out, the famous physicist Einstein was not too hot a scholar at school. In fact, he failed maths initially.

FASCINATING FACT

Other geniuses had favourite toys or games.

The inventor of the telephone, Alexander Graham Bell, had an uncle who would pretend to make his dog speak by manipulating its larynx.

Many years later he remembered this when he was thinking of how to create the telephone.

But something sparked his interest in physics. It was a favourite toy – a magnet. He became very interested in what forces caused the magnet to attract metal. So he started to think and wonder. And he began to brush up on his mathematics. Little by little.

Geniuses are more made than born. Einstein's brain now lies in a glass jar in a University in Mid America. It's no bigger than average, but researchers say that it shows evidence of very rich connections between the brain cells.

Every time you experience something new, or think in a new way, you make more connections between your brain cells. The more connections you make, the more brain capacity you build. **At any age**.

In a real sense, every small step in learning makes you more intelligent. **You create your own brain capacity.**

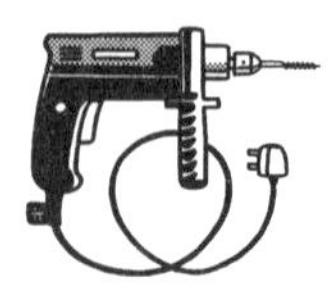

Keep Interested – Ask Questions!

One of the most common complaints people make is that they find it difficult to concentrate.

"How do I get interested?", they ask.

By far the easiest way to stay focused is to continuously develop questions. If you look back to the sort of informal learning situations we all thrive in, active questioning is so often a key feature.

The trick is to write down these questions on a separate piece of paper. They act as a sort of "prodder" – keeping your brain focused on the trainer, teacher or text book, looking for the answers.

"Constant questioning is the first key of wisdom."

Abelard

"I'd rather know some of the questions than all of the answers."

George Bernard Shaw

Try asking general as well as specific questions. Good general questions are:

- How can I use this?
- Do I agree with this?
- Does this assume something that may not be true?
- How does this relate to what I already know?
- If this is true, what else follows?
- What else could the facts mean?

An important tool to winkle out the meaning of what you are learning.

Interrogate!

If you just glance at the sky you might fleetingly notice that it is cloudy. If you really **look** at the sky you will notice how the clouds change shape. You will wonder why the shapes can change so dramatically. That can lead to an interest into how wind and temperature combine to form the various types of cloud we see, e.g. cumulus, stratus or nimbus.

Why does the weather mainly come from the West in the Northern hemisphere? Is the direction of weather reversed in the southern hemisphere? What makes a sunset so beautiful? Why is it made up of reds and oranges?

"Reason can answer questions, but imagination has to ask them."

Ralph Gerard

What? Why? How? When?

If you only glance at a garden, you might notice it is "rather nice". If you really **look** at a garden, you will see the incredible symmetry of a flower, the geometry of a spider's web in the morning dew, and maybe wonder whether there is a mathematical order to nature.

Effective reading is a conversation with the author.

Or you may ask why there's so many colours in nature? If it is just to attract bees for pollination, surely three or four colours would be sufficient? In fact there are thousands of shades of colours in nature for which we do not have even a name.

Why? What? How? Suppose?

You see the point. A surface glance, and you can stay bored with a subject. But the harder you look, the more interested you become. Sometimes you have to initially force yourself to get into the detail – but once you start **really** looking, you get hooked. You start to wonder and explore, and that's learning.

Another way to keep interested is to imagine you are an interviewer. Your job is to make sure the author or lecturer does not get away with woolly statements or half truths. A sort of David Frost of learning!

So keep asking questions like:

- "How do we **know** this is true?" and
- "Is that conclusion justified?"
- "What additional arguments could I think of?"
- "Is this fact or opinion?"
- "Is this logical?"
- "How much evidence is there for what is being said?"
- "Can I think of any (better) examples to illustrate what's being said?"

When you read to answer a question or solve a problem you read with a sense of purpose i.e. with **interest**.

*Assigned text books **can** be boring. If you are turned off by a subject you need to master, seek out a different, lighter, clearer book on the subject.*

The more you know about a subject the more interested you become.

It is very easy to make up your questions. Simply take the main heading of the section and turn it into a question. For example a question to ask about this section is "**Why** should I ask questions?" or "**How** will it help me learn?" or even "**How** do I make up questions?"

When you listen to a teacher or trainer with questions in front of you, you automatically concentrate better.

Use this skill now

EXAMPLE

1. Why is it, or was it, always easier for me to learn Design & Technology and English at school than Science?
2. What's the quickest and best way to improve my memory?
3. How can I use these ideas to overcome my difficulties with Maths and accounts?
4. How does all this apply to my night school class – how can I use it there to help me to learn more effectively?
5. Can I use all this information about learning to help my daughter to tackle her GCSE's?

IMPORTANT

Probably the biggest difference between "natural" or "informal" learning, and "formal" or "academic" learning is this.

In natural learning situations you are almost always able to ask questions, and often there is someone else available to explain it to you.

Learning how to ask ***yourself*** *questions, and how to find out the answers to your own questions by yourself is a key learning skill. A super power tool!*

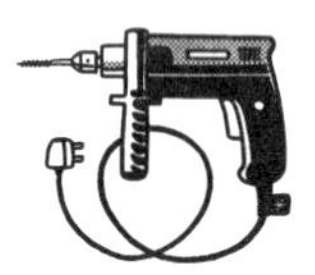

Now ask the questions **you** want answered by this programme.

ACTION

My questions about Accelerate Your Learning	**Examples of general questions you could ask:**
1. ____________________	
____________________	What's the main idea on each page?
2. ____________________	How can I use this? What's the relevance for me, my work and my family?
____________________	
3. ____________________	★ ***THE STAR QUESTION*** ★
____________________	*How can I put this into my own words?*
4. ____________________	
____________________	
5. ____________________	
____________________	

Learn with a friend

You will expand the range of questions you develop by discussing them with a friend. Your discussion will probably prompt further questions that neither of you would have thought of alone.

It All Starts With Your Senses

All new information enters our brain through one of five senses. We either see it, hear it, touch it, smell it or taste it. There is simply no other way for **new** information to get into your mind!

In practice we do not use our sense of taste or smell much in learning unless we are babies, cooks or perfumiers! So to understand the process of learning, it will suit us to say that we have three main ways to take in information. We see it, we hear it and/or we physically experience it.

This all sounds obvious - but there is a big significance here. People differ greatly in **how** they best take in new information. And learning, of course, starts with taking in information.

Surveys indicate that:

35% of people are mainly visual learners – pictures are important to them.

25% of people are mainly auditory learners – talk and lectures are important to them.

40% of people are mainly physical learners – some form of "hands on" experience is important to them.

Of course, no one is, for example, only an auditory learner. We each have a unique combination that we like to use. And we all benefit from learning situations where all our senses are involved.

If the way we are taught does not match the way we like to learn, we start to lose confidence. We haven't failed – we just didn't have a fair chance to learn.

The big significance is this. Teachers naturally have an unconscious tendency to teach in the way they prefer to learn themselves. But all too often the way they instinctively teach is **not** the way that the majority of their pupils like to learn.

A teacher whose style was "sit still, face the front and listen to me" would appeal mainly to the auditory type of learner. The learner who prefers to take in information by listening.

But what would happen to the more visual or physical learner? There would be a mismatch between the teaching style and their learning styles.

The pupils would all too quickly begin to conclude that they were "poor learners". They would begin to lose confidence in themselves. Then the emotional brain would start to feel stressed and that stress would further begin to reduce the information reaching the thinking brain.

The vicious circle would have started.

This is not just theory. Statistics show that four out of five children at age six are confident in their ability to learn. As young children they have been exploring the world with **all** their senses, usually in a very loving and supportive environment.

Then the "rules" of learning changed.

They were asked to sit still. They explored less and were talked to more. Fewer senses were now involved and fewer of their multiple intelligences were engaged. Certainly it was less fun and there was less personal relationship involved with the teacher.

Learning styles and teaching styles need to be ***matched*** *to enable learning to be enjoyable and successful.*

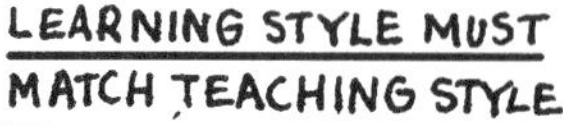

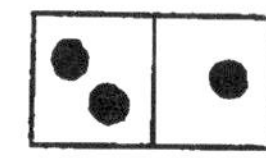

Some learners do well under these circumstances. It suits **their** learning style. Many, though, find that their learning preferences are not met by these conditions.

One survey showed that by the age sixteen, only **one** teenager in five is confident in his or her ability to learn.

The significance of matching up learning styles and teaching styles has only recently been discovered. It does explain a lot of difficulties so many of us had at school and the subsequent lack of confidence felt about learning.

It also explains the common experience so many parents have. Their child does well one year in a subject, but poorly the next or vice versa. Often the reason is a match or mismatch between teaching and learning styles.

Although we cannot normally influence how information is given to us, we **can** choose how we adapt that information to suit our learning preferences.

That is what this Handbook will enable you to do.

WHAT SENSES DO YOU PREFER TO LEARN WITH?

The questionnaire on pages 82 and 83 will give you a good idea of the sense or senses you most prefer to use.

For each question, there are three answers. Circle the answer that most closely represents you. When you have finished, total up the number of responses in each column – visual, auditory or physical. The sense you chose most is likely to be your preferred or dominant learning sense – the sense you are most comfortable using to take in information and to store it.

If you then concentrate on finding and using methods or techniques of learning that match your personal preference, you will be learning in the way that's most comfortable and effective for you. And this may not necessarily be the way that you are taught, so you will have discovered how to make information more compatible to your own brain!

Please note, however, that different learning tasks often call for different approaches. For example, even the most strongly visual learner is not going to learn to ride a bicycle from a diagram! Moreover the questionnaire is mainly to prompt you to think – you'll get most out of experimenting with the techniques that follow and concentrating on the ones that work best in practice.

Situation	Your Preferred Course of Action		
When you ...		**Do you .....**	
	Visual	**Auditory**	**Physical**
Spell a word	Try to visualise it (does it 'look' right)	Sound it out (does it 'sound' right)	Write it down (does it 'feel' right)
Are concentrating	Get most distracted by untidiness.	Get most distracted by noises.	Get most distracted by movement, or physical disturbance.
Chose a favourite art form	Prefer paintings.	Prefer music.	Prefer dance/sculpture.
Reward someone	Tend to write praise on their work in a note.	Tend to give them oral praise.	Tend to give them a pat on the back.
Talk	Talk quite fast, but keep idle conversation limited. Use lots of images , eg it's like a needle in a haystack.	Talk fluently with an even pace, in a logical order and with few hesitations. Enunciate clearly.	Use lots of hand movements, talk about actions and feelings. Speak more slowly with longer pauses.
Meet people	Remember mostly how they looked/ the surroundings.	Remember mostly what was said/ remember their names.	Remember mostly what you did with them/remember their emotions.
See a movie, TV or read a novel	Remember best what the scenes/what people looked like.	Remember best what was said – and how the music sounded.	Remember best what happened/the character's emotions.
Relax	Generally prefer reading, TV	Generally prefer music.	Generally prefer games, sports.
Try to interpret someone's mood.	Mainly note their facial expression	Listen to their tone of voice	Watch body movements.
Are recalling something	Remember what you saw/people's faces/how things looked.	Remember what was said/ people's names/jokes.	Remember what was done, what it it felt like.
Are memorising something	Do you prefer to memorise by writing something repeatedly.	Do you prefer to memorise by repeating words aloud.	Do you prefer to memorise by doing something repeatedly.

Situation	Visual	Auditory	Physical
Choosing clothes	Choose almost exclusively by how they look, how they coordinate, and by the colours.	Take a lot of notice of the brandname, what the clothes 'say' about you.	Chose mainly on how they feel, the comfort, the texture.
Are angry	Become silent and seethe.	Express it in an outburst.	Storm about, clench your fists, throw things.
Are inactive	Look around, doodle, watch something.	Talk to yourself or others.	Fidget, walk about.
Express yourself	Often use phrases like: *I see/ I get the picture/ Lets shed some light on this/ I can picture it.*	Often use phrases like: *That sounds right/ I hear you/ that rings a bell/ something tells me/ it suddenly clicked/ that's music to my ears.*	Often use phrases like: *That feels right/ I'm groping for an answer/ I've got a grip on it/ I need a concrete example.*
Contact people on business	Prefer face to face contact.	Rely on the telephone.	Talk it out while walking, eating, etc.
Are learning	Prefer to read, to see the words, illustrations diagrams, sketch it out.	Like to be told, attend lectures, talk it over.	Like to get involved, hands on, try it out, write notes.
Assemble new equipment	First look at the diagrams/read the instructions	First ask someone to tell you what to do.	First work with the pieces.
	And then your second choice would be to		
	Ask questions/ talk to yourself (A) as you assemble it, and then do it. (P)	Ask them to show you (V) and then try it. (P)	Ask questions (A) and then look at the diagram/instructions. (V)
TOTAL RESPONSES			

Understanding your responses

Visual learners like drawing diagrams, pictures and charts and watching films.

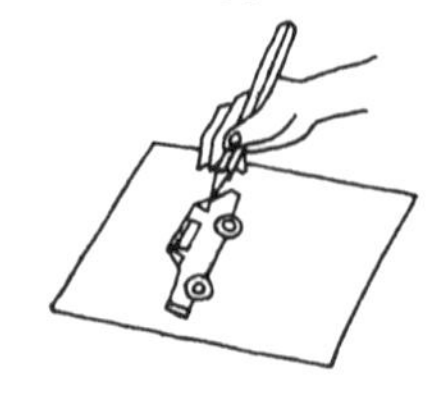

Do you have a dominant or preferred way to access information? Most people have a clear first, second, then third priority. For most people it makes sense to use techniques that 'fit' with your two most preferred senses. Others, who have very strong preferences, will want to use techniques that are very close indeed to theirr ideal sensory mode.

Strong Visual Preference?

You will tend to find it easier to take in new information if it is presented through diagrams, drawings, pictures, charts and films.

You will probably find it easier to learn if you set out to make pictures from new information, i.e. to try to sketch something out for yourself, to draw a plan or a diagram in order to try to help understanding develop. You would also benefit from using visualisation to picture what you are learning in mental images.

Visual/Verbal learners like to read the written word. They like books, posters with slogans, instruction material with clearly written text.

A Visual/Auditory Combination?

You will tend to find it a lot easier to take in new information through the written word, from books, instruction leaflets and posters with clear slogans.

You will probably find it easier to learn if you have accompanying written handouts during lectures or written instructions to support diagrams and explanations. Clearly drawn and labelled graphics are useful to you.

Auditory learners like to hear new information through spoken explanations, commentaries and tapes.

A Strong Auditory Preference?

You tend to find it easier to take in new information through listening to the spoken word. You'll probably find it easier to learn if you hear an explanation, rather than see diagrams or plans. When reading for information, you could read important passages softly to yourself so you hear the words.

Making a tape of something you want to learn, and then playing it back to review the material would be effective for you. So would explaining the subject to someone else. The sound of your own voice makes it memorable.

Physical learners like hands-on learning where they can immediately try things for themselves.

*They like to **do** as they learn, e.g. Writing, underlining, doodling, imagining.*

A Strong Physical Preference?

You will tend to find it a lot easier to take in new information if you are able to act physically. Writing or drawing to record the information as you hear it or read it will probably help.

Copy a demonstration immediately on seeing it, or act out or walk through a series of instructions.

Underlining and highlighting written materials helps learning. You'll find it easier to learn through demonstrations, which you can then copy, rather than through books or explanations.

What works for you

The above test can only be indicative. You should use it in conjunction with a careful observation of what works best for you. Try out the ideas in this section and note the ones that make learning more effective and easier for you.

That's the real test.

Multi-sensory learning can be as simple as:

- Read and visualise the material . . . . you have **seen** it.
- Make up questions and answer them aloud . . . . you have **heard** it.
- Write out the answer to your question and circle the major point . . . . you have **done** it.

Spelling

It has been discovered that good spellers **invariably** bring to mind a image of the word (V) and can 'feel' (P) if it is right. Bad spellers don't use this sequence. They try to check the work phonetically and with English that is a poor predictor of correct spelling!

There's more advice on spelling in the section on memory.

Consequently it is much more productive to teach a bad speller the sequence of V then P, then it is to ask him or her laboriously to memorise the specific spelling of thousands of words. You have then taught the correct principle, and that principle holds good in thousands of different situations.

Teaching and Presenting

Professional teachers, or people who regularly present to meetings, should take special note of the fact that, when you have presented a signficant amount of new information, it is natural for the audience to start to process that information internally.

Listeners with a visual preference will generally start to look up in order to sort out the information visually. Listeners with an auditory preference will tend to turn their heads and look sideways (or down). Listeners with a physical preference will tend to look down and perhaps fidget.

The enemy of understanding is the 'talking teacher'.

John Hunt

To the presenter,all this can look like inattention. Many lecturers will instinctively react by increasing the pace and volume of their talk in an attempt to force attention and 'hammer the point home'. The result is to irritate the audience and to reduce their level of understanding.

A better strategy would be to reduce the pace. This allows the internal processing to take place and time for a 'recap'.

A teacher who comes to recognise that she or he is a primarily visual communicator, will find a much better rapport if she deliberately introduces Auditory and Physical elements into her teaching. Clashes in learning styles versus teaching styles often explain why a child can do poorly one year and then bloom the following year with a new teacher in the same subject.

Getting The Facts To Suit Your Brain

You are now familiar with the idea of taking a book, a lecture or a training demonstration and doing something **extra** that helps you learn in a way that suits you best.

Although some people have very strong learning preferences, "multi-sensory" learning provides the best chance for successful, long-lasting learning for the majority. Multi-sensory learners deliberately engage all their senses as they learn. They **V.A.P. IT**.

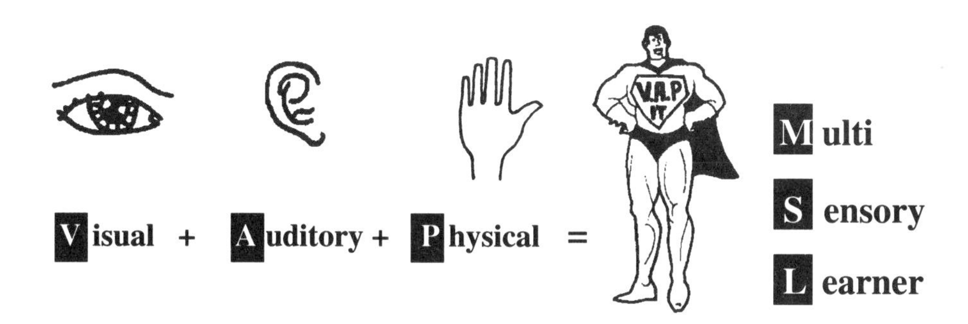

Since we appear to have a separate memory for what we see, what we hear and what we do, the deliberate combination of all of our senses makes for highly efficient learning. So **V.A.P. IT!**

Look back again at pages 4 and 5 of the Introductory Booklet. They indicated that using all our senses together is the ideal.

You already know some excellent ways to use. Here are some more ideas to try. They are extra tools for you to choose, depending on your personal preferences.

Tick it off!

If you have a text book or large instruction manual to tackle, make a light pencil tick at the end of each paragraph that you have fully understood. It is a sort of signal to your brain to lock that information away. What's more you can identify exactly where it was you started to get lost. Just after the last tick!

It is a **good** thing to read and re-read a difficult passage. Sometimes read aloud. Instead of feeling overwhelmed by a whole chapter you can concentrate on understanding small chunks at a time.

Even people who have learned the most complex subjects start with the simple basics and work up.

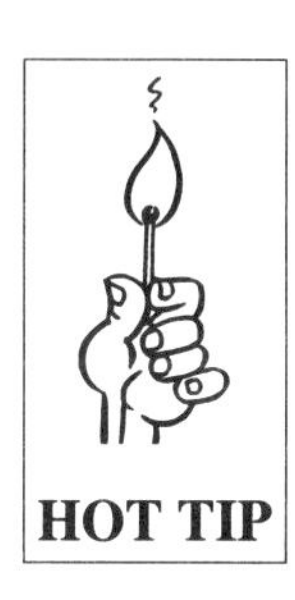

KEEP LOOKING BACK . . .

Every now and then stop and take a short break.

Before you start again briefly review what you have just learned. You "revise" the subject – and get a motivating sense of progress.

. . . AND FORWARD!

If you also flick forward briefly you are setting your brain up for the subject.

It's the equivalent of a warm-up to a runner.

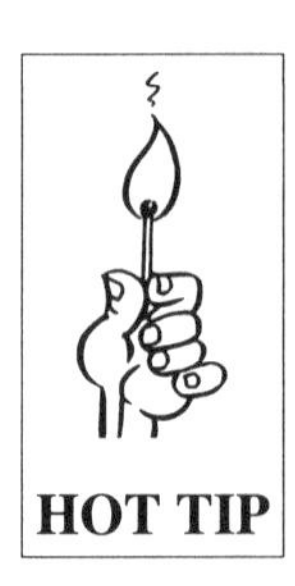

HIGHLIGHTS

Do not highlight or underline the first time you scan read a paragraph or section. Do it when you read for the ideas.

The advantage of highlighting is that when you come to want to review your notes later you only need glance at the highlighted ideas.

Result? You can revise your knowledge of a whole book in 15 minutes or so.

Use a highlighter pen

If the book is your own, using a highlighter can be helpful. When you look back on the material a day, a month, or even a year later – you will have highlighted the important bits of **new** important information.

Notice the emphasis on the word **new**. Many people highlight all the important ideas in a paragraph. That sounds logical, but it isn't. The point about learning is that you are acquiring **new** information or **new** ways of looking at old information.

So to highlight something you already know is only going to increase your work when you come back for a quick review later. And a quick review of what you've been learning is an essential part of really "locking it all down".

Highlighter pens also add colour, which appeals to the emotional part of your brain. The more you use your **whole** brain, the easier you learn.

Read it dramatically

We remember what's dramatic. A pastel floral dress may be pretty, but it probably isn't memorable. A single crimson flower on a black dress would be memorable.

Just as visual images can be memorable, so can sounds. So if a passage is crucial or difficult – try reading it out dramatically. You can use a foreign accent or whisper it. (We often whisper what's important!)

You'll remember it, and it's a great tool for auditory learners.

Tape recorders are great for auditory learners.

Tape your summary notes and play them in the car.

Summarise it out loud

Do you remember the statistics in the booklet? We tend to remember more than twice as much of what we say aloud than of what we merely read.

So stop regularly and summarise out loud what you have read.

Sit quietly and visualise

Most of us need to sit and think quietly over what we have just seen, read or heard. Go over it in your "mind's eye" and make a "mental movie" of it. It's a bit likc an "instant rcplay" in a sports programmc. It hclps to storc thc information in your visual memory.

Walk about while you read or listen

We were usually told at school, don't fidget. That was before we realised that the learners with a preference for physical learning **need** some way to express that preference.

Try walking about. Certainly get up and move every 25-30 minutes. Doodle, underline in colour, jot notes, and make Learning Maps.

If it's appropriate to the subject, draw a chart or graph or even stop and mock up a simple model.

Experiment with how much **you** need a physical element to the way you take in information. For example a desk or table may not work as well for you as a lap board.

A FOG SIGN!

Every now and again everyone gets lost. You just can't figure out what the text means. Develop your own sign for this.

A question mark or exclamation mark perhaps. Put it in the margin then come back later.

Make notes on 'Post Its' or postcards

Stationery shops sell 'Post Its' They are little yellow sheets of paper made up into pads. Each small square sheet has a sticky patch on the back.

Because these yellow 'Post Its' are small, they force you to reduce your notes to a very brief form. The key words jump out at you when you look back at them.

If you stick them all on a large sheet of paper they allow you to sort out your thoughts physically .

Post cards work equally well. And you can stick them on the wall where you learn as reminders.

DON'T IGNORE BOREDOM

Our brains don't work flat out all the time.

If you find you are getting bored, stop, get up, and take a break.

Then ask yourself which aspect of the subject ***is*** *interesting. What is relevant? And switch for a time to that.*

Stop a while!

Has this section given you ideas to make the way you learn more "brain compatible"?

Why not take a few moments to write down the ideas you will use in the future to ensure that the **way** you learn suits your sensory preferences?

Inner speech

Have you ever been in a room where the music was so loud that you were forced to say, " Please turn that noise down – I can't hear myself think". You are revealing a truth. Inner speech is the way we hear ourselves think.

In the same way as we need to manipulate images in our brain in order to imagine, so we need to manipulate spoken words in order to think. One is imagery, the other is inner speech.

Up to about two years old, you make sense of the world through mainly physical means – touching, tasting, smelling.

Then you talk aloud as a means of organising your thoughts. (The reason that young children talk so much is that they **need** to talk in order to think.)

Finally you learn to organise your thoughts inside your head without talking aloud – i.e. inner speech.

It follows that when you have a difficult problem, it pays to "back track" down this developmental progression. So you would first try thinking about the problem. Then try talking it through aloud. Then try solving it physically – "walking" through the problem or drawing out a diagram or making a model.

There is a parallel progression for the visual sense. Children will first deal with real physical objects, then they will recognise pictures that represent the object. Finally they will accept symbols for the objects – i.e. letters or words.

If you want to prove this strategy for yourself try the problem on page 139 now!! ☞

Once again if a problem is causing difficulties you should "back track" from the symbols i.e. words. Draw diagrams or charts.

Of course you can combine the "back tracking" strategies. Deal with a difficult abstract problem by visualising it in a diagram, talking it outloud **and** finding a way to represent it physically. The progression would be:

ABSTRACT ➜ TALK ALOUD ➜ VISUALISE ➜ PHYSICAL MODEL

Learning Maps

You will have noticed that we have been using LEARNING MAPS to summarise information for you.

Learning maps have many advantages. They present ideas in a visual form. The information is presented all on one page, clearly and concisely. Only the core ideas or key words are used.

The map shows the connections between ideas in a very visual manner. And because they are visual, they are easier to picture later in your "mind's eye". They therefore help make learning memorable.

Many learners find they can take information in all at once when it is presented in a learning map.

Learning Maps are fast to produce, easy to read and easy to remember.

The essential rule in making a learning map is **only** to use **key words**. Key words are the essential words which – when you read them – remind you of the whole idea. The words that get to the heart of the meaning.

Key words are usually nouns, and since nouns are names of things, they are easier to remember. The aim in effective note-taking is to strip away all the unnecessary words. It's like digging for gold. You get rid of all the surrounding earth to expose the nuggets of valuable information.

Most people take notes that contain **far** too many words. That is a mistake because:

- You waste too much time writing it out in the first place.
- If you write too much you will be concentrating more on the words than on the **meaning** of what the author, teacher or trainer is saying.
- You waste too much time re-reading the notes later.

If you have pages of notes you have to re-read the things you know, as well as the things you have yet to learn properly.

You don't need many words to remember – as long as they are. . . THE KEY WORDS.

IMPORTANT

The secret is to read ideas – not words.

The Learning Maps in this book are "professionally" produced. They work just as well when they have fewer pictures – see the Super Skills Supplement.

This will show you how to make your Learning Maps work for you.

KEY WORDS UNLOCK A LOT OF MEMORY

How to make your own Learning Map – A summary

1. Draw a picture, symbol and/or write a phrase in the centre of the paper to stand for the topic.

2. Strip away everything except the key words. This is the most important rule.

3. Take the main ideas associated with the topic and let them branch out from the central idea. Express things with a picture, a symbol or key word or phrase on your map. Use only one or two key words per idea. This is the second most important "rule".

4. Stop and think. Add new thoughts like branches on a tree. Put questions on areas you don't understand properly.

5. Organise your map – you may want to group some ideas that seem to go together, draw lines and/or arrows to represent connections between thoughts.

6. Usually you will now want to redraw your learning map. Don't resent this – it is a good way to help it stick in your long-term memory.

7. Use as much colour and as many symbols and pictures as possible. Our brains find these memorable. Aim to make each page of these notes look different.

8. Use bold and capital letters.

9. Don't crowd the page – leave space.

10. Use the paper horizontally – it gives you more space.

11. Use one side of the paper – so you can use your learning maps as posters – or spread out a number of them in sequence.

It ***is*** *essential to experiment with learning maps.*

The first time you try anything it feels strange and may even take a little longer.

That's true of riding a bike or driving. First it seems odd – gradually it becomes familiar and natural.

So persevere – it's worth it.

ACTION

Experiment with Learning Maps.

First pick a topic you are very familiar with, such as yourself – your life, family, interests, job etc.

Then experiment by making a learning map about the skills of learning.

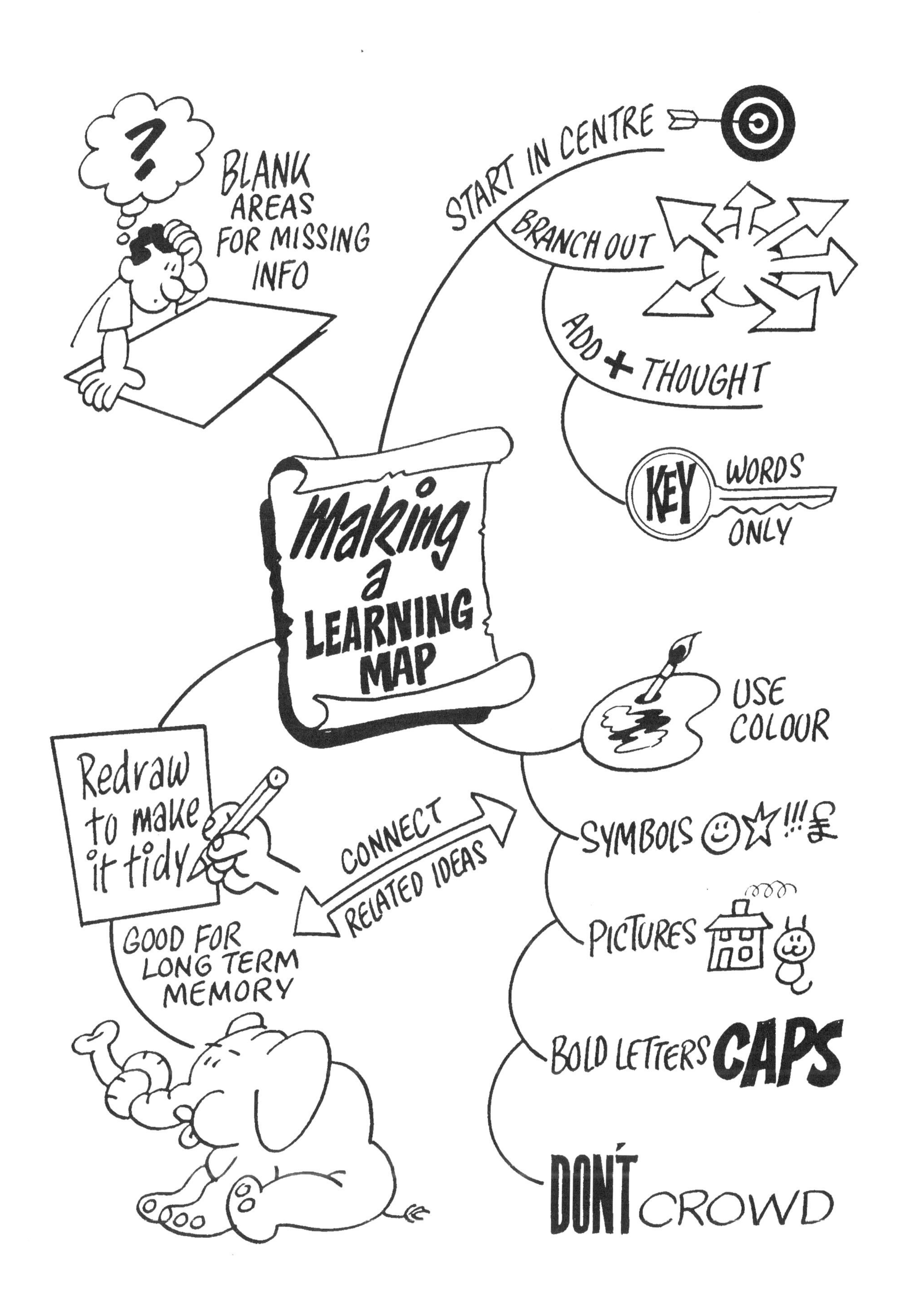
Making a LEARNING MAP
START IN CENTRE
BRANCH OUT
ADD + THOUGHT
KEY WORDS ONLY
USE COLOUR
SYMBOLS ☺☆!!!£
PICTURES
BOLD LETTERS CAPS
DON'T CROWD
CONNECT RELATED IDEAS
Redraw to make it tidy
GOOD FOR LONG TERM MEMORY
BLANK AREAS FOR MISSING INFO
?

The main advantages of Learning Maps

They are fun.

The information is all on **one** page. The theme, the core idea, is at the centre, and the ideas that follow from that main theme are clustered around it.

Because the information is visual, it's possible to take it in all at once, and after a little study, to picture it in your mind's eye. This is especially easy when you have constructed the learning map yourself.

You can add new words (ideas) anywhere, at any time.

Because you get used to reading or listening for only the essential **ideas,** you learn to cut out irrelevant material. Great for concise reports and getting to the **meaning** of the subject.

You can jump about from one "idea cluster" to another and literally "see" the connection between one idea and another.

You can pick out, and concentrate on, the areas or ideas you haven't yet fully understood .

If the book you are reading – or the lecture you are listening to – wanders about without an obvious or clear theme, you will be able to see the connections between ideas much more clearly when you have set them down in a learning map form.

*A learning map is a tool to turn ideas and facts into an easily remembered **VISUAL** pattern of words.*

*It is also a tool to allow **you** to create a logical order for those ideas. Powerful stuff!*

You begin to impose **your** order on other people's messy thoughts! The "shape" of the argument will literally begin to emerge. The definition of "meaningful" is something that fits into a shape or pattern or order that **you** create. You turn someone else's ideas into your own.

If you need to rework your original draft learning map, the very act of finding more logical ways of grouping the ideas together helps you figure out their meaning.

And because they now become **your** ideas, they are easier to remember.

You can actually summarise a whole book on a one page learning map. That makes them great for revising. Your brain is forced to fill in the extra information "triggered" by the keywords and, as we know, the more you use your brain, the better you learn.

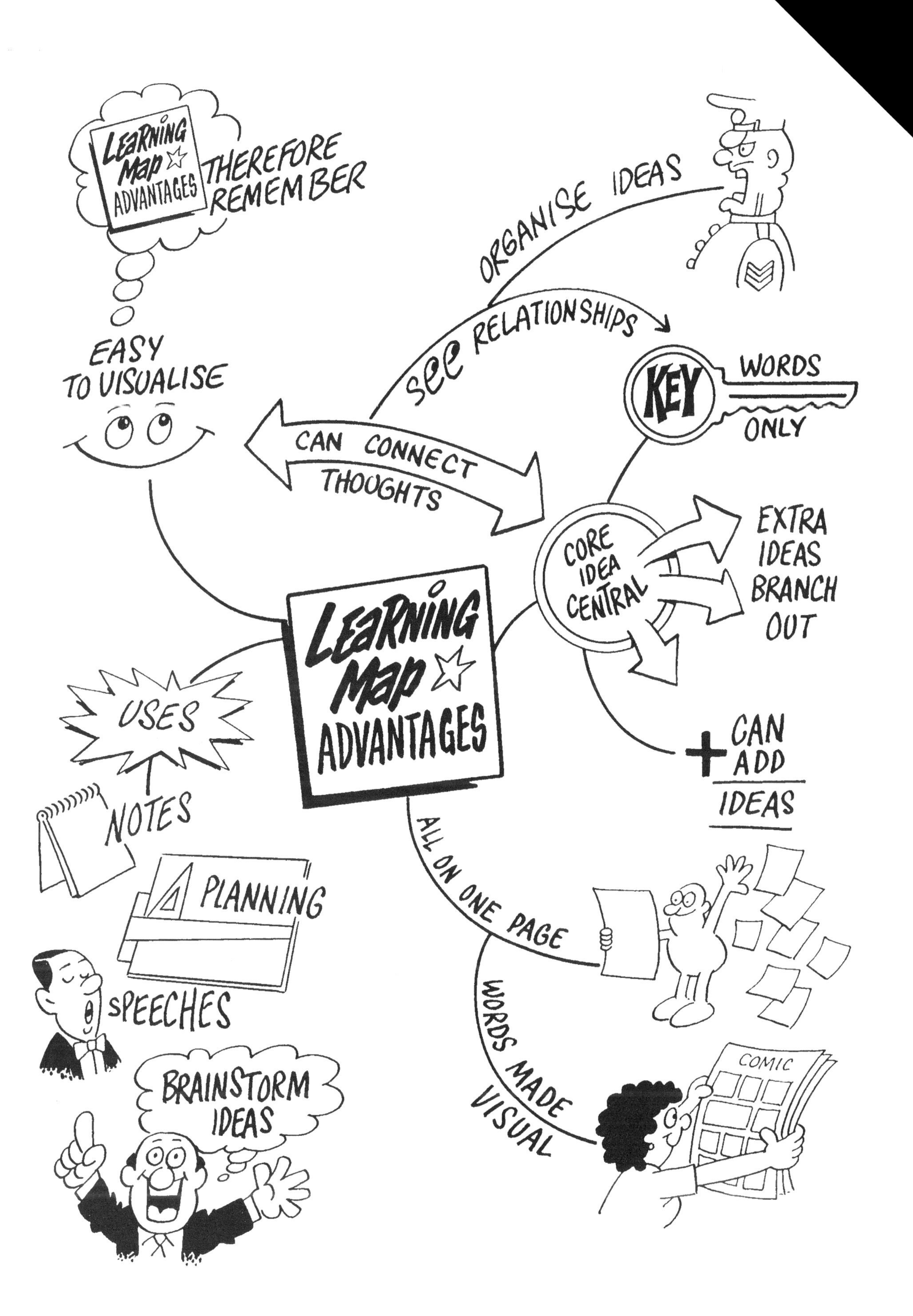
LEARNING MAP ADVANTAGES
LEARNING MAP ADVANTAGES THEREFORE REMEMBER
EASY TO VISUALISE
ORGANISE IDEAS
SEE RELATIONSHIPS
KEY WORDS ONLY
CAN CONNECT THOUGHTS
CORE IDEA CENTRAL
EXTRA IDEAS BRANCH OUT
CAN ADD IDEAS
USES
NOTES
PLANNING
SPEECHES
BRAINSTORM IDEAS
ALL ON ONE PAGE
WORDS MADE VISUAL
COMIC

Learn with a friend (or two)

It is always helpful to share your thinking with someone else. If you have some fellow students or colleagues also tackling this programme, you could agree on a topic for a learning map and either produce a map together or produce your own maps and compare the end results.

Learning Maps can also be very useful to plan speeches, presentations, agendas, reports or papers.

Use this skill now

In the next part of the programme we are going to look at your seven intelligences and how you can use them to explore a new subject. Flick through the section now for a maximum of about five minutes. Don't read the section, just browse.

ACTION

Now map what you know about the seven intelligences.

As you were mapping what you knew about the seven intelligences, questions were almost certainly forming in your mind.

- Were there areas you knew nothing about?
- Were there aspects that puzzled you and you wanted clarified?
- Perhaps there were things you totally disagreed with and you wanted to challenge?
- Did you wonder how to use the information in a practical way?

*There is an important difference between taking notes and **making** notes.*

Taking notes implies copying down other people's thoughts and opinions.

***Making** notes is when you turn their information into your **own** thoughts and opinions.*

ACTION

Write out your questions beside the relevant area on your learning map. You can show where you need further information by putting in a question mark or a blank area to be filled in on the map.

The pay off

You have now effectively prepared yourself for reading the next section on exploring what you are learning. You will now be geared up to look for the answers that fill in the gaps in your knowledge.

In other words you are beginning to know what it is that you **don't** know!

Try To Imagine It All In Your Own Mind

You've learned a whole number of tools to make sure you take in information in a way that suit your own preferences.

We learned to:

- Create the big picture first – to skim read to get a feel of the subject.
- Sketch out what you already know and therefore pinpoint what you don't know.
- Create some questions you want answered. To pretend to "interrogate" the author of the text or the trainer.
- Break every learning task into manageable chunks.
- Create and use Learning Maps.
- Tick off what you've understood.
- Use a highlighter pen.
- Read important bits aloud and dramatically.
- Walk about and take breaks.

ACTION

Now go back over the above list, but this time do not just read each idea, but stop and **visualise yourself doing each one.**

Don't move on until you've made a really good image of yourself doing it – a mental movie. When you've pictured each one **separately,** make one final sequence in your mind, where you do all of the ideas one after the other.

Finally check back on the list and see how many you have now remembered.

If you really want to jump ahead you could try one more very effective strategy. You could go back to the list **and number each idea**. Then make a final image in your mind, where you go through each idea in number order, adding in the ones you forgot before. Try it!

If you have really had a go – (and remember the only good learning is where you get stuck in!) – I strongly suspect you were able to remember more of the ideas this last time, than the first time.

What does **that** tell you about effective learning?

T.W.A. CREW ACHIEVE 100% PASS RATE WITH MENTAL IMAGERY

Airline flight attendants need to know the location of over 60 pieces of emergency equipment.

T.W.A. attendants boosted their pass rate from 70% to 100% with the following sequence.

1. *They toured the plane noting the safety locations.*
2. *They filled in the location diagrams from memory.*
3. *They checked them against the master diagram.*
4. *They then sat, closed their eyes and visualised the original tour in their mind's eye. They then filled in the location diagram again.*

*How can **you** add mental imagery the next time you learn something?*

There is a complete section on using imagery to learn in the "Super Skills Supplement".

The Final Skill – Knowing When To Stop!

DEALING WITH DISTRACTING THOUGHTS

If thoughts keep intruding on your learning, don't ignore them.

Acknowledge the thought, get up, move about and breath deeply. Then let the thought go as if it were a balloon floating upwards.

There are times in every learning situation when you simply can't make head nor tail of it.

The right approach is not to struggle grimly with it for hours and end up with a bad case of depression, but to move on and come back later.

The next section of the book may be much easier to understand. More importantly, it may contain clues that help you understand the bit you got stuck on.

You rarely have only one chance to understand something. So write down what you **don't** understand, and come back to it in a day or so.

Or write it down and ask a friend or expert for help.

. . . But come back later!

Researcher E. M. Gray searched for years for the one **single** factor that all successful people shared.

Here it is.

Successful people simply do the things that failures don't like and can't be bothered to do.

Successful people don't necessarily like doing them either! But their vision of success is stronger than their inertia. **They stick at it.**

Check what you have learned about Stage Two

1. Why is it vital to get an "overview" of the subject?

2. Sketching out what you already know about a subject helps you in two main ways. What are they?

3. Why does it help you to concentrate when you ask yourself questions as you learn?

4. If it is a big project, how do you tackle it?

5. What does V.A.P. stand for?

6. What is the essential rule in making Learning Maps?

7. List some advantages of Learning Maps?

8. What should you highlight with a highlighter pen?

9. Why does summarising something outloud help?

Answers on page 215

A Learning Map Of Stage Two

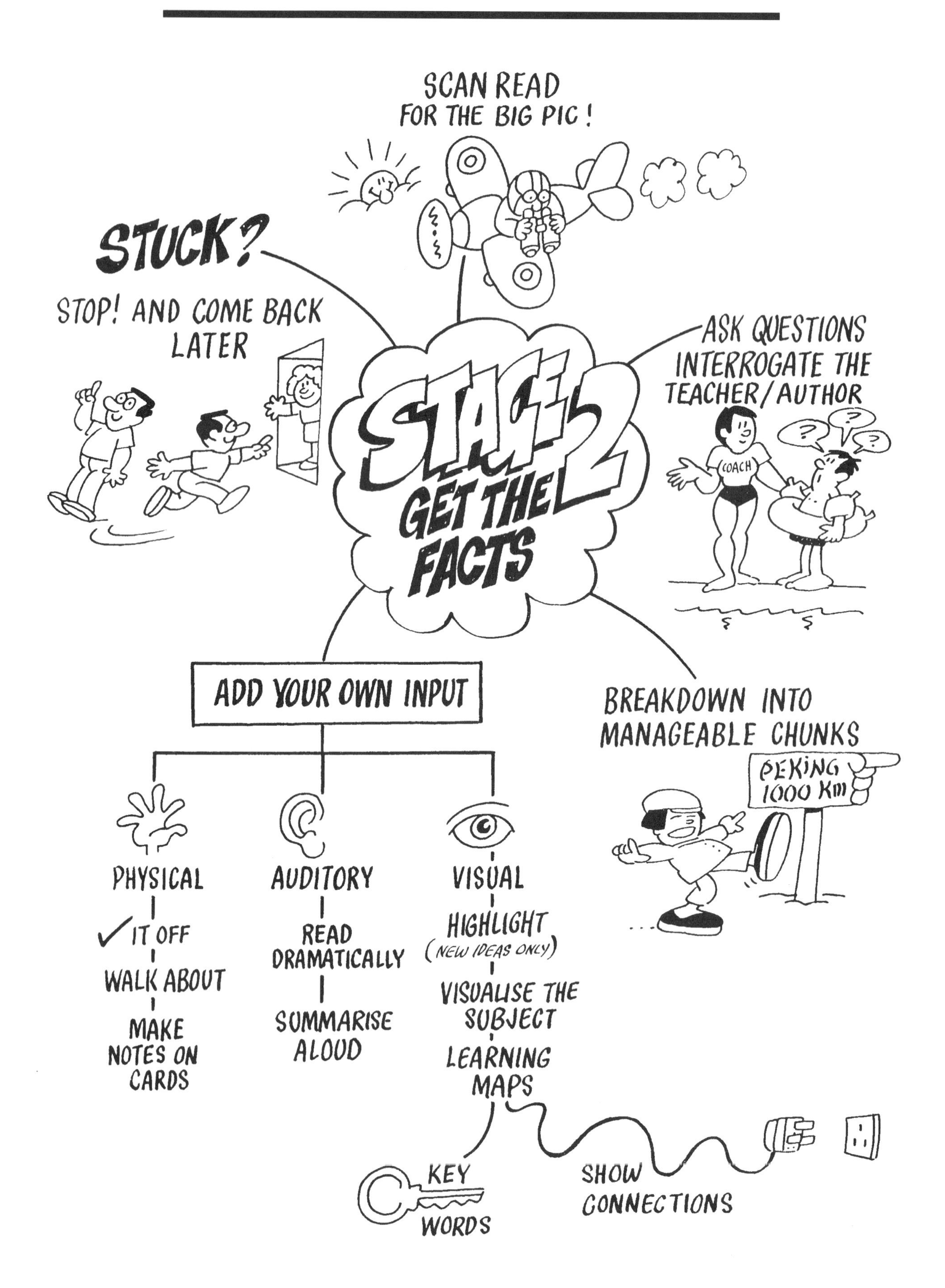

A time for reflection

If you are a learner at work:

- The main ideas from this section that I will use in my job or career are:

  ____

  ____

- Although I originally did well in my studies, I can see that there are ideas here to learn even better in future. They are:

  ____

  ____

- I didn't achieve everything I could have done at school. But I could start to realise more of my true potential, if I:

  ____

  ____

- The following ideas will enable me to help the people I am responsible for:

  ____

  ____

- As a parent, the ideas that can help my children are:

  ____

  ____

If you are a student:

- The ideas I am going to use to help me learn more effectively are:

  ____

  ____

- Some of the ideas are worth talking over with my friends. They are:

  ____

  ____

- I really feel I would like to discuss some of these ideas with my teacher or tutor. They are:

  ____

  ____

Stage Three

Explore The Subject

The Penalty Of Surface Understanding

Taking a subject at face value, without stopping to explore what it really means, can be costly.

When J. Edgar Hoover was head of the American FBI, he received a poorly typed memo. It was about the potential danger of terrorist groups causing trouble in the major US Cities.

Hoover was very particular about neat memos. So he was cross that the letter he had received was sloppily typed and the margins were badly laid out.

He therefore wrote "Watch the Borders!" across the top of the page, and returned the memo.

Two weeks later there were hundreds of FBI agents staking out the Mexican and Canadian frontiers!

Brains are like muscles

When you deliberately use your range of intelligences you exercise your brain. Like your muscles, your brain power literally does grow with use. That's why intelligence is not fixed. You are an important influence on your own brain.

Learning is not something that's done to you. **Only you can do it.** The best any teacher can do is provide an atmosphere and materials that encourage you to want to explore and learn. And help you overcome difficulties. The actual business of learning is entirely **your** responsibility!

We will regularly be using a phrase I have borrowed from an inspirational writer called Dr. Robert Schüller ...

IF IT'S TO BE, IT'S UP TO ME!

How To Turn Facts Into Knowledge

Someone once defined a lecture as a means of transferring the notes of the lecturer to the note pads of the students – without it entering the minds of either!

For true learning to take place you have to **do** something.

Turning the facts you have acquired into knowledge that you really understand and can **use** is the job of the third stage of learning.

You now need to deepen your understanding of the subject – by exploring it in one or more ways that suit your unique combination of intelligences.

When you do, you will be using your **full** range of mental powers. It's whole brain, Accelerated Learning. You start to convert theoretical data to useful, practical, personal knowledge.

There is a good example in the margin.

REMEMBER

One bite at a time!

This section has a lot of new ideas to try.

Take it bit by bit. Read a bit, think about it, and try out the ideas. There's no rush!

"You can't pick up knowledge, ready-made as if from a supermarket shelf. You need to make your **own** knowledge."

Derek Rowntree

THEORY INTO KNOWLEDGE

If I were to tell you that an acre is 4047 square metres, that's data. Easily forgotten, because it doesn't ***mean*** *much.*

If, instead, you were to discover that an acre is about the size of a football pitch, that's knowledge. You have related it to something you know.

You probably used your visual intelligence by picturing a football field.

You took something that was just abstract information and turned it into meaningful and useful knowledge.

That is a pretty good definition of learning!

Explore What You Are Learning With Your Seven Intelligences

Howard Gardner and colleagues at Harvard University have demonstrated that when your range of intelligences are put to good use, learning ability is greatly enhanced.

Each type of intelligence represents a different way to explore the subject. A different ability to call on when you need to tackle a problem.

Your seven intelligences

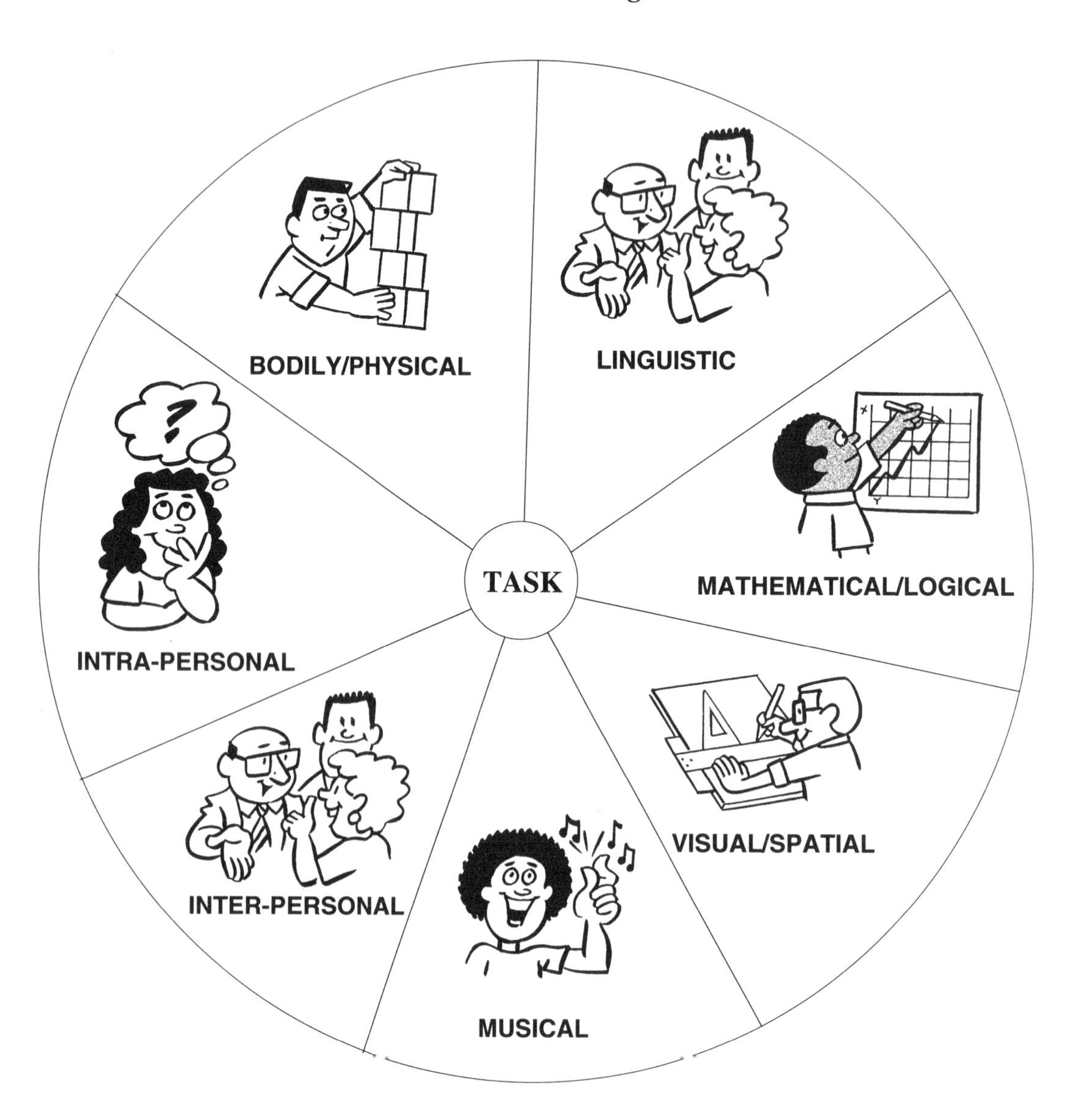

A new view of intelligence

This new way of looking at intelligence tells us three critically important things:

- **Intelligence is not fixed**. A person can excel in one situation and appear to be highly intelligent. Yet he may be at a complete loss in a different situation. The absent-minded professor illustrates this well!

- **"Intelligence" is simply a set of abilities and skills**. You can develop and improve your intelligence by learning to use your abilities to the full. This programme gives you the "tools of the trade" to develop these skills.

  Intelligence is demonstrated by what people do and achieve. Become a good "doer" and you'll **show** your intelligence.

- **You need to work to use, develop and improve your intelligence** – it can't and won't happen without effort on your part.

80% of what we know about the human brain was discovered in the last 15 years.

It overturns some previous assumptions.

Accelerate Your Learning aims to give you access to a wide range of skills for learning. The more "tools of the learning trade" you possess, the more flexible and competent a learner you will be.

The Learning Map overleaf is our summary of the information we've given you on the seven intelligences. You may have already made your own learning map about the seven intelligences. Why not compare the two?

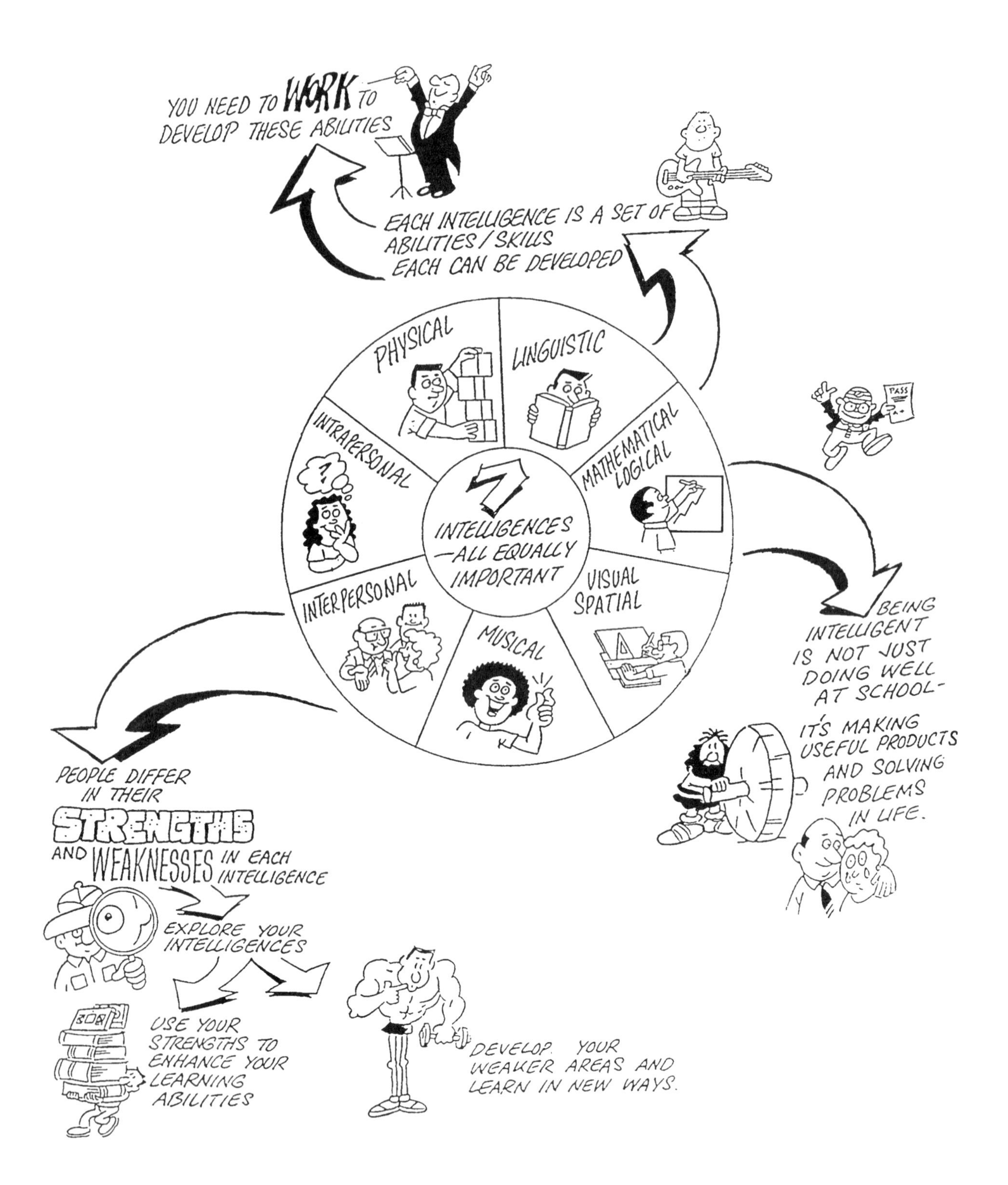

Consciously using your **full** range of intelligences leads to balanced learning – learning that not only suits your current strengths, but that also enables you to develop and grow as a person.

Using your full range of intelligences will also prompt you to think in new ways. The result is that you can become more creative.

Exploring Your Seven Intelligences

Earlier in this Handbook you thought back on some previously successful learning experiences – which types of intelligence did you mainly use during those experiences? You may like to look back.

Now write your first conclusion below.

ACTION

I feel my strongest intelligences are:

____

____

Now transfer the above conclusions to the SEVEN INTELLIGENCES PROFILE on page 115.

IMPORTANT

You may discover further strengths as you explore your learning potential through this programme.

What you will discover about yourself in these explorations describes you at this moment – ***all the intelligences can be enhanced and developed.***

You do this by shading in those segments of the innermost circle that correspond to your strengths. For example, somebody who considered she was strongest in linguistic, musical and bodily/physical intelligences would shade in the following segments of the innermost first circle.

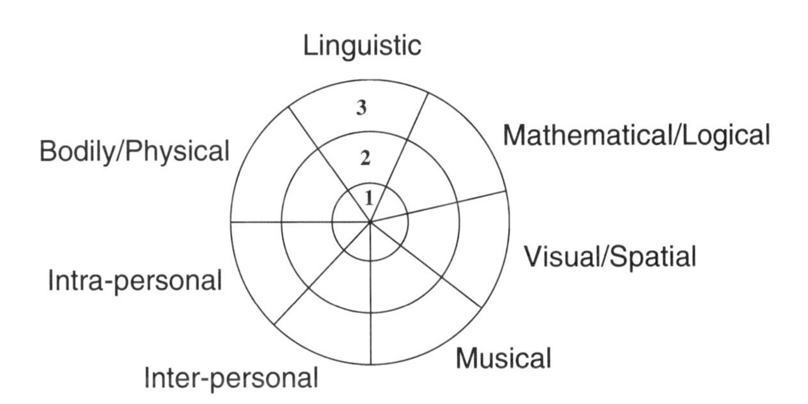

The explorations that follow in this section will allow you to complete the whole profile and build up a picture of your **current** strengths for learning and thinking.

Exploring what you are good at

The following activity helps you explore the subjects, jobs and/or situations in which you excel. What type of problems are you able to solve? What are you able to make or do that other people value?

Competence in these subjects, or jobs or situations may have come naturally to you or you may have had to really work at developing the skills involved. The fact that it is possible to develop such skills proves that abilities are not fixed.

You learn more about a road by travelling down it, than from all the maps in the world.

ACTION

Read through the activities on the next page and record (tick) what you are good at. If you are good at an activity that is similar to one that is listed, but your particular expertise is not actually mentioned – then add it to the printed list and tick it off.

When you have ticked off those activities you are good at, you should see a pattern.

The more activities you tick the stronger you will currently tend to be in that particular type of intelligence.

Exploring a subject in different ways ensures you really understand it.

(Tick what you are good at)

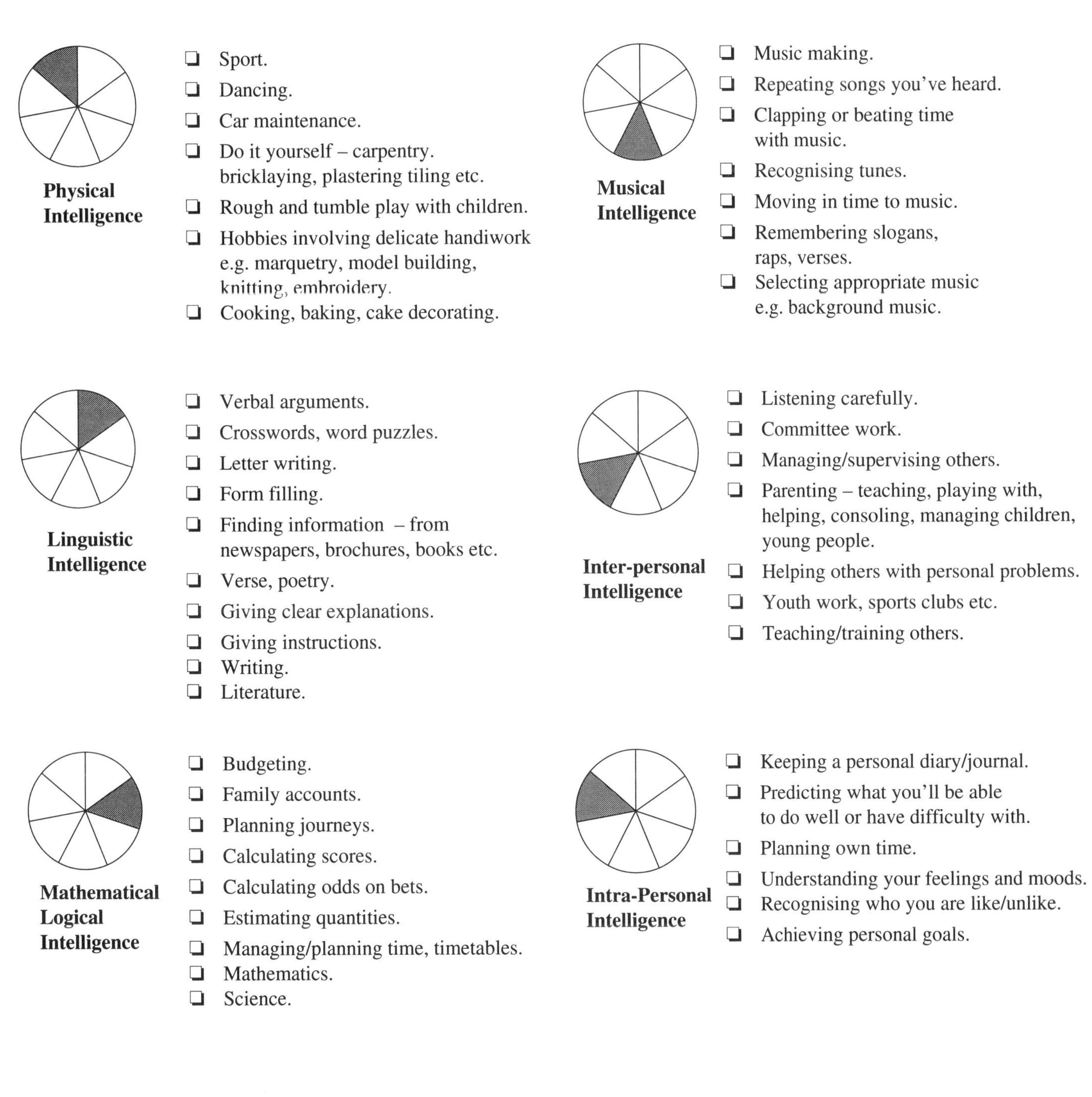

Physical Intelligence

- ❑ Sport.
- ❑ Dancing.
- ❑ Car maintenance.
- ❑ Do it yourself – carpentry. bricklaying, plastering tiling etc.
- ❑ Rough and tumble play with children.
- ❑ Hobbies involving delicate handiwork e.g. marquetry, model building, knitting, embroidery.
- ❑ Cooking, baking, cake decorating.

Musical Intelligence

- ❑ Music making.
- ❑ Repeating songs you've heard.
- ❑ Clapping or beating time with music.
- ❑ Recognising tunes.
- ❑ Moving in time to music.
- ❑ Remembering slogans, raps, verses.
- ❑ Selecting appropriate music e.g. background music.

Linguistic Intelligence

- ❑ Verbal arguments.
- ❑ Crosswords, word puzzles.
- ❑ Letter writing.
- ❑ Form filling.
- ❑ Finding information – from newspapers, brochures, books etc.
- ❑ Verse, poetry.
- ❑ Giving clear explanations.
- ❑ Giving instructions.
- ❑ Writing.
- ❑ Literature.

Inter-personal Intelligence

- ❑ Listening carefully.
- ❑ Committee work.
- ❑ Managing/supervising others.
- ❑ Parenting – teaching, playing with, helping, consoling, managing children, young people.
- ❑ Helping others with personal problems.
- ❑ Youth work, sports clubs etc.
- ❑ Teaching/training others.

Mathematical Logical Intelligence

- ❑ Budgeting.
- ❑ Family accounts.
- ❑ Planning journeys.
- ❑ Calculating scores.
- ❑ Calculating odds on bets.
- ❑ Estimating quantities.
- ❑ Managing/planning time, timetables.
- ❑ Mathematics.
- ❑ Science.

Intra-Personal Intelligence

- ❑ Keeping a personal diary/journal.
- ❑ Predicting what you'll be able to do well or have difficulty with.
- ❑ Planning own time.
- ❑ Understanding your feelings and moods.
- ❑ Recognising who you are like/unlike.
- ❑ Achieving personal goals.

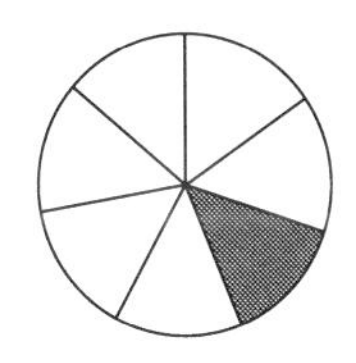

Visual/Spatial Intelligence

- ❑ Map reading and navigating.
- ❑ Using diagrams and plans e.g. engine diagrams.
- ❑ Self-assembly furniture.
- ❑ Driving, parking.
- ❑ Planning gardens.
- ❑ Art.
- ❑ Dressmaking.
- ❑ Model layouts e.g. train sets and model making.

ACTION

Now transfer your conclusions to the intelligence profile on page 115. In other words shade in the segments which represent your current strengths in the second or middle circle which is labelled "results from exploration 2".

The typical characteristics of each intelligence

We have selected five characteristics that describe people who are strong in each intelligence.

The characteristics chosen give you a good flavour of each intelligence, rather than a complete description. You may like to add ideas of your own based on your growing understanding of the ways in which each type of intelligence shows itself.

ACTION

Read through the following page and tick the boxes beside the characteristics that describe you.

❑ **Tick boxes that describe you.**

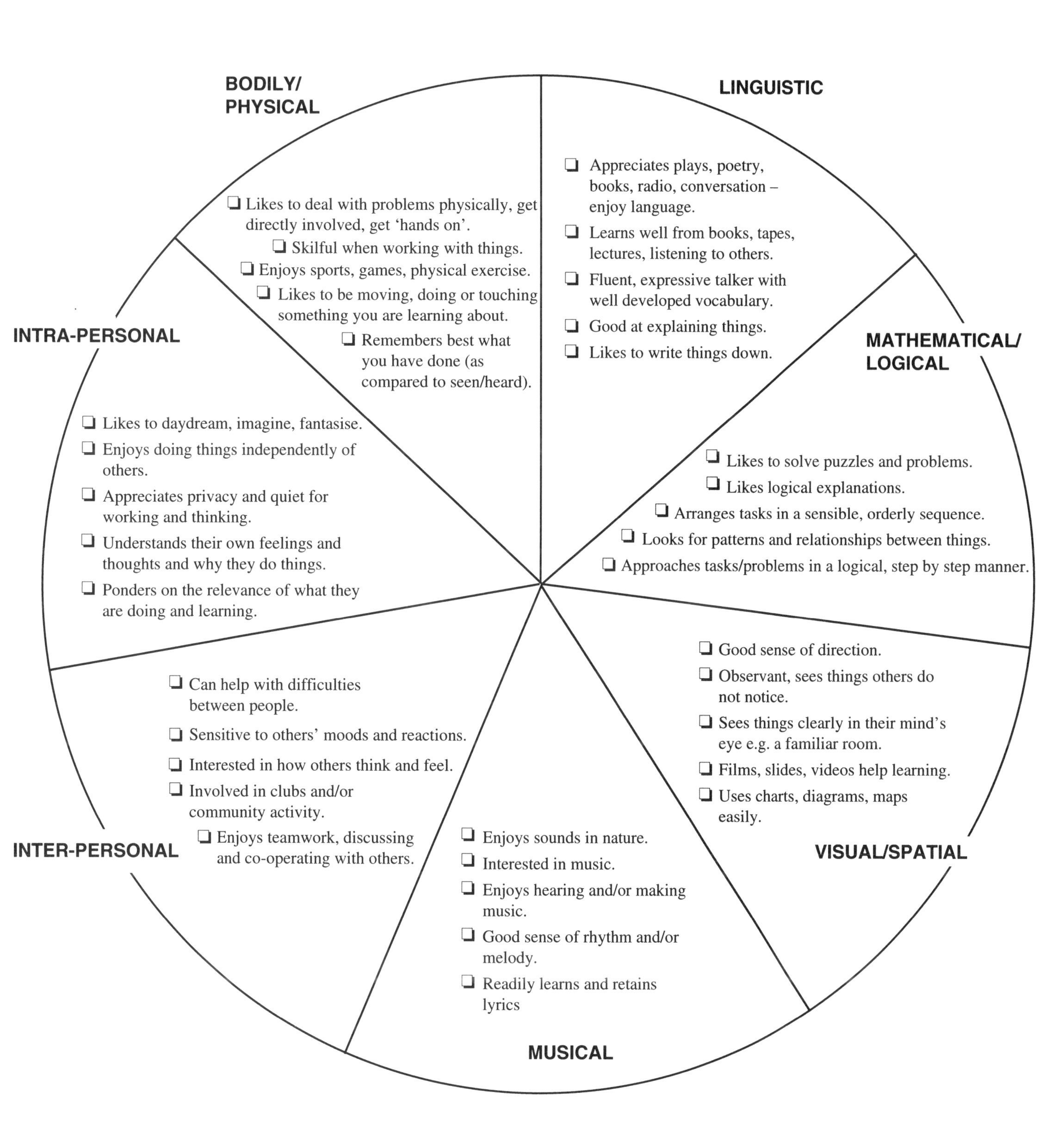

How to use the exploration you have just completed

By comparing the number of ticks you have made, you will have further information on your preferred or stronger intelligences.

If you have shaded four or five boxes in a segment, it is likely that this is currently an area of strength for you.

ACTION

Transfer your findings to your Intelligences Profile on page 115 by shading in the intelligences which seem to be your strengths. Use the outer circle to do this.

Use your Interpersonal intelligence to think and learn

Get together with some colleagues who are also working through this programme. Share your findings and compare your profiles with them.

Have a member of your family or a friend complete one of the wheels for you. Then discuss both your own **and** his/her view of your strengths.

A Current Profile Of Your Strongest Intelligences

Each type of intelligence offers you new ways to explore the problem.

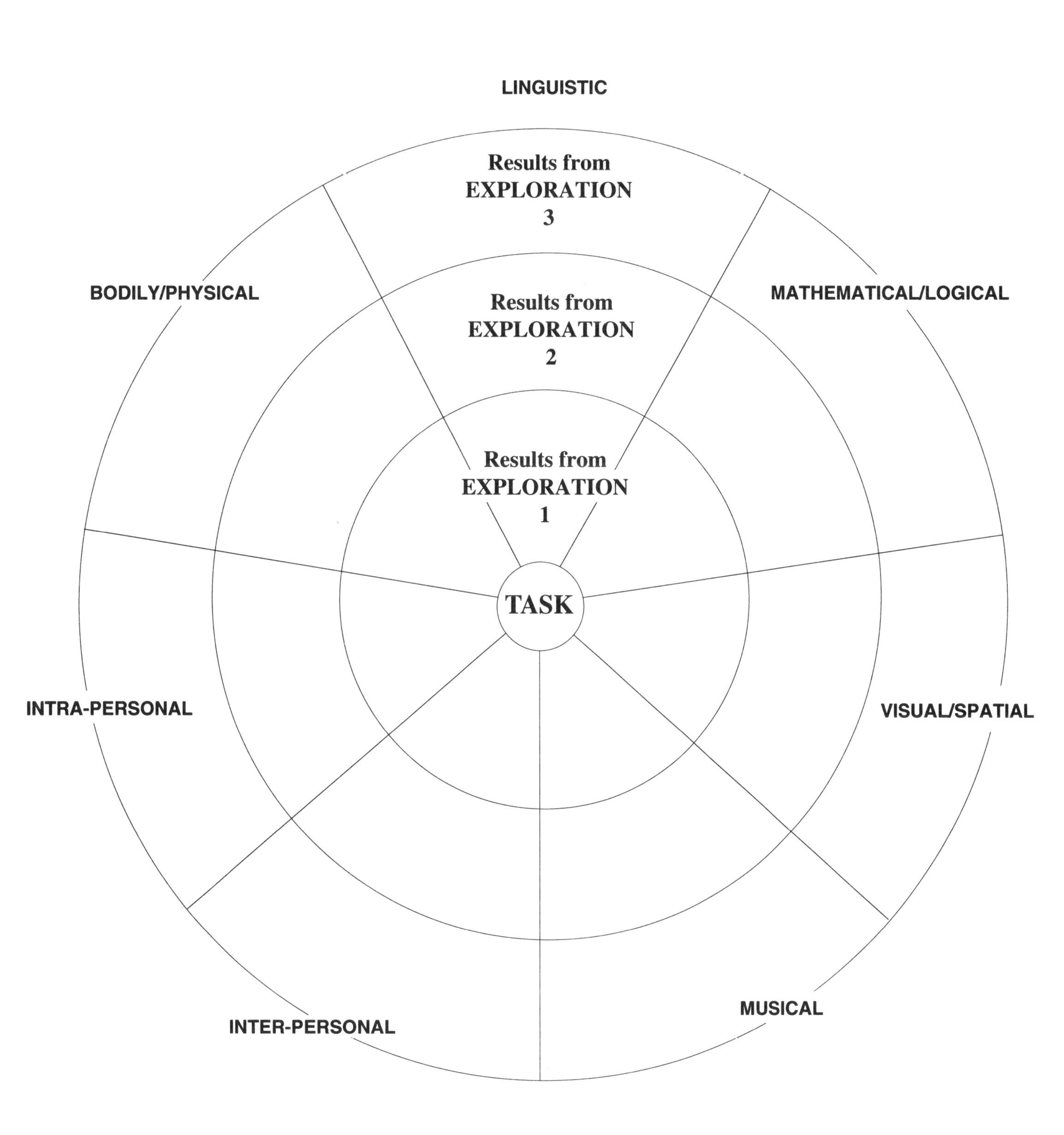

Each type of intelligence represents a different way to explore the subject

¿

- *Does this make sense?*
- *Does this help explain my own feelings towards school and learning?*
- *What relevance does this have to me and my family?*
- *How can I **use** this information?*

***Remember**: A key skill in learning is continuous and active questioning!*

"A mind stretched to a new idea never returns to its original dimension."

Oliver Wendell Holmes

"When everyone thinks alike – nobody thinks much."

Dee Dickinson

Howard Gardner – the Professor of Education at Harvard who came up with the important idea of multiple intelligence – makes a critically important point.

Our schools (and training rooms) typically teach to involve the linguistic and mathematical/logical intelligence. So if your brain is naturally set up to be good with words and figures, you will do well in formal education.

If you like a teaching style that reveals the subject bit by bit in a logical step-by-step manner, you will like the way most text books and lectures are put together.

But this approach – typical of formal teaching and learning – is mostly directed to just two types of intelligence, i.e. "linguistic" and "mathematical/logical". If that's the way your brain naturally works, you're lucky. If it doesn't, school may be a tough experience, because it mostly offers a "single" chance to understand.

It is therefore what Howard Gardner calls "the single chance theory of education".

What about the people who prefer – and often **need** – other ways to explore the subject? Howard Gardner answers that they are not well served by the way we normally present information at school. So they achieve less than they could.

Yet give them the chance to also use other types of intelligence and they can blossom.

This is the "Multiple Chance" theory of education and it's what our work at Accelerated Learning is all about.

When you are more aware of the unique make-up of your brain and therefore know how to use it best, you can become a highly proficient learner. It takes effort, but there's nothing to prevent you or your children achieving anything you set out to. Anyone can learn anything – given only time.

To repeat two themes from this programme.

THE LIMITS TO LEARNING ARE LARGELY SELF-IMPOSED

and

IF IT'S TO BE IT'S UP TO ME

Using your strongest intelligence

You can use your strongest form of intelligence to explore what you are learning. To bring what might otherwise be theoretical or abstract ideas to life. To create "deep" rather than "surface" learning.

Look back at the intelligence profile you have been building up. It will begin to indicate your current strengths.

In the next section you will be able to try out activities that enable you to explore a subject using your particular strengths.

But try to use all Seven Intelligences!

A powerful way to learn is to use as many of your intelligences as practically possible. This way you experience what you are learning in a "well rounded" way.

Take something as common as learning to drive. The pictures below demonstrate how you could use your range of intelligences as you learn to drive.

Learning to drive using the seven intelligences

Bodily/Physical

Practising the skill

Linguistic

Reading up on advice

Mathematical/Logical

Working out braking distances

Intra-personal

Encouraging yourself

Inter-personal

Asking advice from the instructor

Musical

Put some key facts into a jingle

Visual/Spatial

Manoeuvring into a parking space

Explore *Accelerate Your Learning* with your Seven Intelligences

Active exploration is the secret of effective learning .

The next few pages introduce you to seven valuable learning tools or activities. Each activity relies heavily on one of the seven intelligences. We call them activities, because their function is to get you **actively** to explore what you are learning.

Take an experimental approach over the next few pages. Try out some ways to learn that are very different for you – you may be surprised at what your experience reveals.

"Thinking is the hardest work of all. Perhaps that is why so few choose to do it!"

Henry Ford

You will see how to use **each** of these seven different ways to develop a real understanding of this Learn-to-Learn Programme. These ways, however, can be used to explore anything you want to learn.

Facts only turn into learning when you think about them in a way that gets your brain ACTIVELY INVOLVED.

Think of your intelligences as your team.
You are the player manager whose job it is to get the best out of them.

Seven Ways To Explore What You Are Learning

Read each suggested activity below. Then see how we have used each activity to deepen our understanding of *Accelerate Your Learning*.

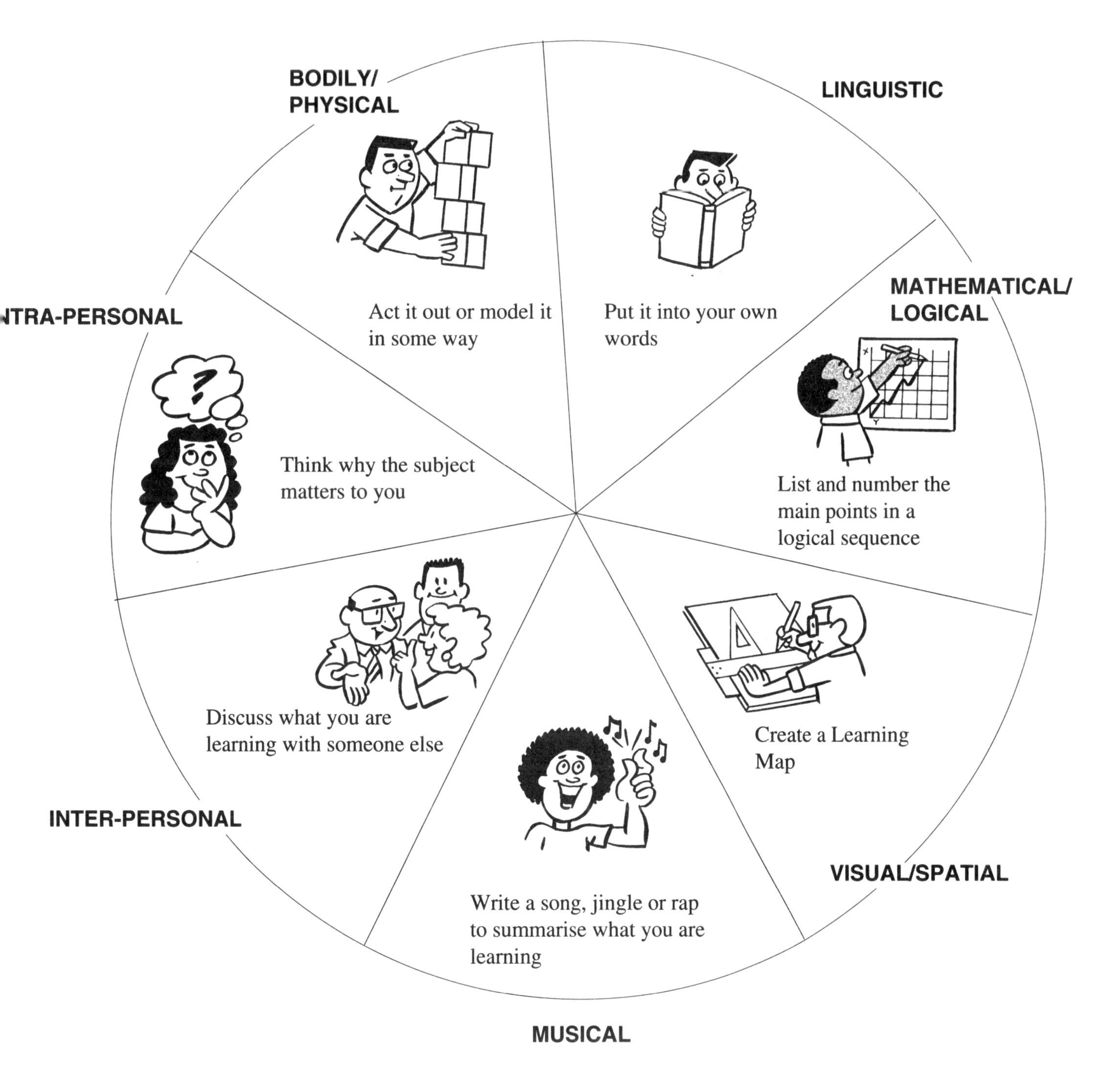

Note: Some of these ways to explore the subject will seem comfortable. Others might seem "odd" to you. That's because you **do** have a personal learning style.

Your friends may like what you dislike – and vice versa. That's what individual preference is all about.

Mathematical-Logical exploration

List the key points of what you are learning in a logical numbered sequence.

Applying your logical intelligence to this programme could also involve:

- *Considering what proportion of your time to give to each of the main tools for learning over a particular project.*
- *Recording how often you used each of the seven intelligences in the course of a week – and which activities were most enjoyable and successful. The record could be put on a graph.*
- *Trying out each of the 14 ideas on page 142 and grading them to establish which* ***combinations*** *seem to suit you best.*

Selecting the important points of a subject means that you need to think carefully about what you are learning. If your understanding is fuzzy, this will become immediately obvious. It is an excellent way to make sure you really get to grips with a new topic.

When you also rank these points in order of importance, you start to think even more deeply about them.

The content of *Accelerate Your Learning* can be summed up in a logical, numbered sequence. There's one at the very end of this handbook on pages 210/211.

ACTION

Think about what you have learned about the process of learning in this programme. List the important key points, and then sort them out into a logical, numbered sequence.

On the opposite page is another important way to use your logical intelligence.

Analyse what you are learning

When you are systematic, you use your logical intelligence. When you are analytical, you also use your logical intelligence. So when you use a system to be analytical, you are **really** using your logical intelligence!

When you analyse what you are learning, you examine it in detail. You look for the essential parts of it. You don't take it at face value, you explore it in depth. And that's effective learning.

To think analytically about your subject isn't difficult – but it isn't necessarily natural either! That is why the following systematic approach helps. It comprises a group of questions.

1. **What ASSUMPTIONS are being made?**

   Has anything been taken for granted?

   Has anything been left out?

   Has the author used an isolated example to make a general or sweeping conclusion?

2. **What's the EVIDENCE for this?**

   Are we dealing with facts or opinion?

   If it's opinion – can I trust the source?

   If it's fact – is this always true? What other explanation could there be?

   If this is true, what else follows?

3. **Can I think of a good ILLUSTRATION or example of this?**

   Does this fit any other category or class of things I'm familiar with?

   Is what I'm reading or hearing consistent with my experience?

4. **What OPINION or conclusions can I draw about this?**

   Are they justified?

5. **What are the UNIQUE points in this?**

   What are the key and new points?

   What is essential to know – and what is just padding?

These questions help make sure you always stop and think. It's all too easy to accept your first reaction or thought. But initial conclusions may not always be right.

What's more, authors, teachers and trainers are human. They are not always right either!

The value of a systematic approach is that it makes life easier. You know that if you follow the plan you will achieve a good result. A bit like assembling a model from a kit or painting by numbers!

Make the use of these questions a habit of mind.

You can copy the questions onto a card or even onto a poster for your wall.

Use them until they become automatic.

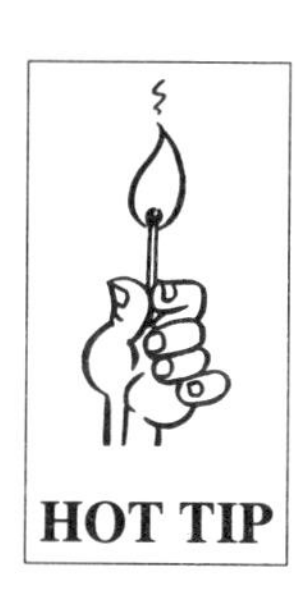

You can remember these questions by recalling the vowels of the alphabet A.E.I.O.U. It reminds you of the first letter of the key words:

***A**ssumptions?*
***E**vidence?*
***I**llustrations?*
***O**pinion?*
***U**niqueness?*

IF YOU ARE NOT ASKING QUESTIONS,

YOU ARE PROBABLY NOT LEARNING!

Linguistic exploration

Put it into your own words

It is extremely hard work to learn a series of words written by somebody else. Think of how difficult it can be to learn a poem or the lines of a play.

Learning the words "parrot fashion" certainly does not mean you understand them. But putting what you have heard or read into your own words, **does** need you to understand it.

ACTION

To make sure you have really thought about and therefore understood *Accelerate Your Learning* put the main ideas into your own words.

Here are three possible ways to begin. Choose one and try it out.

1. "Brainstorm" all the things you feel you have learned. To brainstorm simply write down or say into a tape recorder everything you can think of. Avoid being critical of ideas – write down or say everything that comes to mind.

   Next, skim through the pages of this book to jog your memory and add further thoughts. Be careful to put these into your **own** words – don't copy out or merely repeat chunks of the text.

   You will now have a list of points. You can next organise these points in any way that is meaningful to you. For example, you can draw out what you consider to be the five most important points, or put them on postcards.

Linguistic intelligence is important because the more vocabulary you have, the more accurately you can express yourself.

It helps to jot down every unfamiliar word you come across and look it up as soon as you can in a dictionary.

The black leader Malcolm X educated himself in prison doing just this.

He became highly successful as a public speaker.

Linguistic intelligence can be used in imaginative and fun ways. You could describe this whole programme in a series of limericks.

A start might be:

"A trendy young student called Jane
No longer thinks learning's a pain
She . . ." etc., etc.

Or you could lay it out in the style of a newspaper front page.

The headline might be:

"Learning Secrets Exposed"

"You can unleash the genius in you through Six Stages of Learning says . . . " etc., etc.

2. Imagine you are either writing a letter to a friend or telling a friend about *Accelerate Your Learning*. This friend has never had the opportunity to find out or think about learning. In fact, her experiences of school and learning have not been enjoyable, although you know her to be an intelligent and practical person.

   It is important that you use straightforward language. You can write, talk out loud, or even record it into a tape recorder.

3. Fill in the following box with a short summary of what you have discovered about each of the three stages of learning we have introduced so far.

   Making a summary is a very useful skill because you have to reduce what you have learned to its essentials. That means deciding what's important.

   To do that you have to think deeper about the subject and that ensures you remember it well.

You need words in order to think. If children lack an adequate vocabulary they are forced to express themselves in other ways.

Sometimes they hit out at the world, because they feel they have no other way to communicate than physically.

That's why reading to young children and conversation is so important. TV is a passive medium and cannot give the depth of language skills that reading provides.

Getting in the right state of mind to learn

____

____

____

____

Getting the facts to suit myself

____

____

____

____

Exploring what I'm learning

____

____

____

____

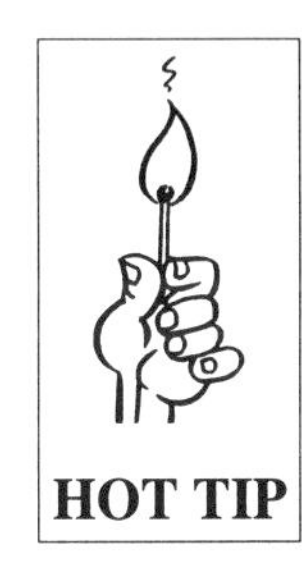

When you are reading, stop at the end of ***each*** *main section, lay your book aside and recall the key ideas in your own words from memory.*

Then, if relevant, express any new opinions or conclusions that have been triggered by that section.

Intra-Personal exploration

Interest creates motivation

What is your favourite hobby?

I doubt if anyone had to nag you to learn it! If you are interested in a subject – you're motivated to learn. But supposing you are faced with a subject that currently you think is, frankly, boring. What then?

Keeping a diary or a "learning log" that records your reactions to the ideas in this programme is a good intra-personal activity.

Record how it has helped you towards your goals.

How may your future be changed by it?

Do the ideas fit into your personal beliefs about people?

Researcher Droba tested students' memory for paintings. Some just looked at the paintings, others were given information about the painting and the painter. The latter group remembered the paintings twice as well.

They remembered better because they created their own interest in the subject by digging deeper. They did not take it at face value, they explored the subject on a **personal level**.

Here's what **you** can do.

Whatever the subject you are learning, ask or read about the background – especially the human interest. If the subject is art, music or drama, what was in the creator's mind? What did she or he do differently from anyone else before? What new technique did she evolve?

If the subject is history, you might visualise the characters of the people who created the political or social changes. Approach it like a novel, looking for the ambition, power struggles, weaknesses, strengths, loves, hates and quirks of character of the people involved.

Get your emotional brain involved. Ask yourself which side you would have supported, allow yourself likes and dislikes. Contemporary history is easier to absorb because we each have a mental picture of the characters involved, and we form our own opinions of them! TV and newspapers make them "real".

If you start thinking of history in terms of characters, headlines and political skulduggery, it also becomes real. If history were taught like that, it would be most people's favourite!

How about maths, can there be an emotional interest in this subject? Indeed there can. Just look at the margin!

How about technical subjects or learning in an industrial environment? The same advice applies. Look for the human interest. Who developed the system? What were their initial difficulties and failures? Why is the system designed the way it is?

I doubt if there's a subject in the world that hasn't got its devoted followers. People are avid collectors of Mesopotamian nose flutes, and others are addicted to computer programming.

The secret of creating interest in a subject is to look for something that has **personal** significance for you. Anything to create that first "spark" of interest. Then the genuine interest follows.

People make subjects interesting. The unusual makes subjects interesting. Unexpected connections make subjects interesting.

Above all we become interested when we can answer questions like:

- Why does this matter to me?
- How can I **use** this idea?
- What significance can I find in this for me?

So if you haven't been doing this, go back over the text so far and apply these questions to the ideas you have already learned.

One final tip, why not ask your teacher, lecturer or trainer what they find interesting about the subject you are studying. After all, they chose to do it full time!

Or seek out someone who is excited by the subject and ask them what intrigues them. Every subject can be made to have personal interest, and that's the secret of motivation.

If world population is growing at 2% – how many years will it take before the total population doubles?

Quick answer *35 years.*

Why? Because there is a simple, useful math rule. Divide any percentage rate of growth into 70 to find out the time it takes for something to double.

70 ÷ 2 = 35

World population was 5,000,000,000 people (i.e. five billion people) in 1987.

If it were to grow at 3% rather than 2%, then the time it would take for our planet to have to accommodate yet another five billion people would be just over 23 years.

So by year 2010 the world population would, on average, be increasing by ***200 million*** *people* ***a year****.*

That's like adding a new France and a new Germany ***every year*** *and trying to find food, water, clothes, schools and jobs for them.*

When mathematics is used to explore ***relevant*** *issues it becomes an exciting subject.*

Why should you divide into 70%? Why not 80% or 60%? Are you asking questions as you learn?

.70 is the natural log of 2.

Visual/Spatial exploration

Creating a Learning Map

Throughout this programme we have summarised the information we have given to you on Learning Maps. These are even more helpful aids to learning when you have constructed them yourself.

You can lay out the information in a way that makes sense to you. Then you can reorganise it to show the connections that are important to you.

ACTION

Make a large Learning Map which summarises all that you have learned until now. You will be able to add further information as you read on.

Sometimes all you need is a brief sketch. Many mathematical concepts are easier to solve when you find a way to visualise them. Try the problem in the margin now.

There are **lots** of ways to explore a subject visually. Depending on appropriateness, consider making up a coloured poster, a cartoon, a video, or a timeline. Use symbols instead of words.

Above all try visualisation and read **SUPER SKILL THREE** on learning through imagery in the Super Skills Supplement.

THE BOOKWORM

Four volumes of an encyclopaedia stand side-by-side on a shelf, the correct way round.

Volume I is on the left, Volume IV is on the right.

Each book is 4" thick and the covers are 1/16" thick.

A bookworm starts eating at page one of Volume I, and eats its way through to the last page of volume IV.

How many inches did it chew through?

Answer on page 33 of the Super Skills Supplement.

Inter-personal exploration

Have a discussion

Discussing what you are learning is an excellent way to check your understanding of something new. You will also gain from the other person's experiences and insights. This is particularly helpful if that person will ask you questions and even challenge your opinions.

You use your Inter-Personal Intelligence when you consider how this programme could help your family, your school or your community.

Talk about *Accelerate Your Learning*

Find some colleagues at work or at school who are also following this programme. Set aside some time when you can get together and talk about what you are learning. Here are three possible ways:

Co-operative learning is such a ***vital*** *skill that we have a whole section on it – Super Skill Module Four in the Super Skills Supplement.*

1. Informal discussions are valuable. These can often happen at coffee or meal breaks.

   You can casually discuss what you have discovered with others in this way . . . "I found this interesting . . . what do you think?"

   It is easier to involve people in discussion about something when you ask them about **their** personal experiences . . . "Did you find when you were at school that . . . ?"

2. Get a discussion going by asking for something with which your colleagues disagreed. One of the others is likely to agree with it, and the discussion has started.

All this illustrates an important point. We too often consider that learning needs to be formal, as at school, in lectures, training rooms or from books. This is quite untrue. Some of the most important learning of all can take place around a family dinner table.

You could do nothing more helpful for your family than to regularly discuss what each of you is doing, and **how you can all learn from these experiences**.

STUDY BUDDY STRATEGY

Here's a proven way to learn better.

a. Team up with a colleague.
b. You each agree to learn the same chapter or section independently.
c. When you next meet, you both summarise what you have learned to each other and note and discuss differing interpretations.

You both learn better!

Problem swap

Here's a practical way to create solutions to the sort of everyday problems that inevitably arise at work.

Take a lunch hour and get together a small group. Have some blank post cards ready. You each take a post card and write on it a problem that is bothering you – large or small. Then the whole group devotes 10 minutes to coming up with a solution.

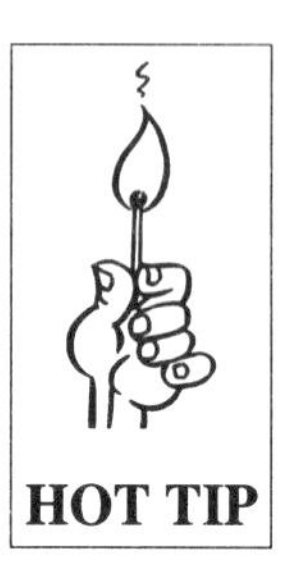

Yes, you could theoretically just sit and discuss your problems without organising it in this way – but the truth is you rarely do.

This simple bit of informal team work works wonders. And if you persist with the idea, you'll find that problems will increasingly be sorted out by this type of informal group rather than "officially" – or alone.

To parents – Involve your children

Ask your children what they think of some of the ideas in this programme. Let them tell you their feelings and experiences about learning. Do they get on well in a particular class. Why is that? Does the way it's taught match the way they like to learn? Do they find any of these ideas useful?

TO STUDENTS

If you are a full time student involve your parents. Discuss the implications of this programme with them.

Don't be too alarmed if they initially react negatively. It's a sad fact that many children who are experiencing what Howard Gardner calls the "single chance" approach to schooling are switched off by any mention of study, because they feel they cannot succeed. **They are they very ones who will most benefit from these ideas**.

Bodily/Physical exploration

"An ounce of experience is worth a ton of theory."

Benjamin Franklin

Act out or Role play what you are learning

Physical movement helps many people to get involved in what they are learning – they can't think for long while they are sitting still.

Acting out something that you are learning allows you to turn theory into something more memorable.

"Role play" helps you explore what you are learning by acting out a new role in a safe situation. Role play can also help you understand other people through acting out their roles. It helps you see the world from their point of view.

Sometimes the role play can be actual. For example, acting out words and phrases when you are learning a foreign language is very effective.

"Why," said the dodo, "the best way to explain it is to do it!"

Lewis Carroll
Alice in Wonderland

Role Play to explore Accelerate Your Learning

Some role plays that might work for you:

1. You are at school and now able to explain to your teachers how you and your friends would like to learn.

   Get into the role and say and do the things you imagine you would do.

2. You are appointed as the spokesperson for your workmates. You have to explain to the trainers at work how you would all like to learn about a new procedure.

   Suggest ways to learn that will ensure you all enjoy the experience and will remember the content better.

   Get into the role and say what you would say, aloud, as if you were really in the situation. Try out your rehearsal on someone else and ask them for constructive criticism.

There's lots of ways to physically explore a subject.

If you were trying to explain this Accelerate Your Learning programme to a child, you could make up a sheet with all the tools of learning on it, and then cut it out to make a jigsaw.

By assembling the jigsaw, the child would see how the elements all "fitted together".

You could make up a cube with the six sides representing the Six Stages of Learning. On each side write out the appropriate tools for that stage.

Then use the cube as a dice. Roll the dice and see if they can describe what to do at each stage.

The power of writing

Writing is a physical exercise, so we should not be surprised that when we write something down, we learn it better. We have added a physical element (writing), to sight (reading), and sound (inner speech).

If you go into any library, you will find that a remarkable number of successful people kept diaries and journals and wrote detailed letters to their family and friends.

Researcher Dr. Win Wenger poses a question, "Did these outstanding people record their observation of things from early childhood **because** they knew that some day they were going to be great?

Or did the practice of recording their own observations develop in them the characteristics which led to their becoming great?".

Worth thinking about!

Role Plays are ideal for learning history.

Imagine you are the character you are learning about. What would he or she say, do, feel, see?

*Talk about that person in the first person. "**I** am Henry VIII, **I** have six wives".*

Musical exploration

Write a song, jingle or rap

Do you find remembering the lyrics of a song or an advertising jingle easier than remembering a piece of text? The melodic and rhythmic patterns of the music really ease the task of remembering.

When you express what you want to say in a concise and rhythmic way, and then fit those words to a melody, it makes the words highly significant and memorable. You have to really **think** about what you are learning to do this. Which makes for effective learning.

Music is a much more powerful learning aid than we normally appreciate.

Think how many songs you know – yet have never consciously learned.

Often you only need to hear the first few bars to trigger the words of an entire song.

Write a song, jingle or rap about Accelerate Your Learning

You can use your musical intelligence to help you with this programme. Take the ideas you find most relevant and important to you, and create a song, jingle or rap with them.

You do not have to be musically gifted to do this. Here are some ways to get started if you feel it's too difficult.

1. Choose a memorable jingle from a radio or TV advertisement. Take some key information from this programme and try to fit it to that jingle.

2. Listen to some raps and notice how the words are just chanted to the rhythm of the music. At first just try reading bits of *Accelerate Your Learning* in a similar rhythmic way. If you feel comfortable with that, you can try to make up some simple verses to fit the rhythm of the music.

   Children seem to be able to do this very readily. If you have children or know children that like rap music, ask them to make up a rap about something, and you'll soon see how it's done.

3. Make up some simple verses about the content of this programme. The rhythmic quality of the words will help you learn.

4. Take a well-known song and write your own words to the familiar melody.

Real estate agents have to learn complex new European rules. One enterprising exam candidate set the rules to music and she passed top of her class.

Learning and singing songs in a foreign language is an effective and pleasant way to expand your vocabulary.

Singing or chanting mathematical or scientific formulae works well too.

It is interesting that exploring a subject through their musical intelligence is the one that most people find a little "strange". Yet years ago, before TV and newspapers, it was common for knowledge to be passed down in rhymes and songs. Even today, the Maoris of New Zealand pass down much of their history in song.

Some of the most memorable advertising messages are presented in jingles, and years later you still remember them. And it is through rhyme that we remember the days in each month – "Thirty days has September" etc.

Modern technology allows us to see which areas of the brain are working at any one time. The **same** area of the brain is functioning when someone is engaged in mathematical reasoning as when they are performing and reading music.

Research from test schools – including the FACE school in Montreal – indicates that when one hour a day of music, art and drama is added to the timetable, grades in ALL the other subjects can be improved by as much as 20%.

Active involvement in music and the arts is a **centrally** important element in raising confidence, enjoyment and actual grade standards in schools.

But are we taking enough notice of this fact?

When you study the arts you develop your ability to perceive and think in new ways. The arts are forms of communication – so you develop skills of interpretation. They provide insight and wisdom, not just information.

Learning through the arts builds the inner spirit as well as the brain and our understanding of human values.

Let's Stop And Digest All This!

What's the betting that you are sitting there thinking "Hey – I thought this was supposed to make my life easier! What a lot of work. No way!"

This **is** a long section. Because the stage where you really explore i.e. think about what you are learning, is so important. And we are introducing a lot of new ideas in a short time. But that is precisely what many learning situations challenge you to do.

You already have the answer. Take frequent breaks, and remember that you are deliberately working your way through a lot of alternatives.

You would rarely use **all** these activities in any one learning situation. At the most you would probably use one or two. But you need to know and try them all in order to settle on the ones that are most suitable for **you.**

So take your time. Try one activity a day if you feel like it. *Accelerate Your Learning* is designed to help you improve the rest of your life! It doesn't matter if it takes you six weeks to go through. Time is not the issue – becoming a very effective learner is!

HOW COMMITTED ARE YOU?

The Spanish explorer Cortez had a novel form of motivation for his men. When he landed on the shore of Mexico he set fire to his own ships and presented them with the choice "Win or die"!

Thus was born the phrase: "Burning your boats behind you."

Success has a lot to do with determination and persistence.

The duckling

This is another true story. A little girl visited a farm with her father. Out of a clutch of a dozen eggs, all had hatched but one.

"I'll help it, Daddy" said the little girl and gently cracked the egg open. In the night the duckling died. The struggle to be born is a vital part of the process of creation. It simply doesn't work without effort.

This programme requires you to spend effort now, so your learning will be easier later.

Nothing worthwhile gets created without persistence.

Nothing worthwhile is learned in "five easy lessons"!

The very word "worth*while*" means that the subject is "worth a *while*".

"The only place where success comes before work is in the dictionary!"

Vidal Sassoon

Luck favours the backbone, not the wishbone!"

Seven More Ways To Explore The Subject

There are many ways to explore a subject. Perhaps you are now coming up with ideas of your own in order to use your brain power more fully.

Here is a further "Intelligence wheel" describing another seven ways to explore and learn – one for each intelligence.

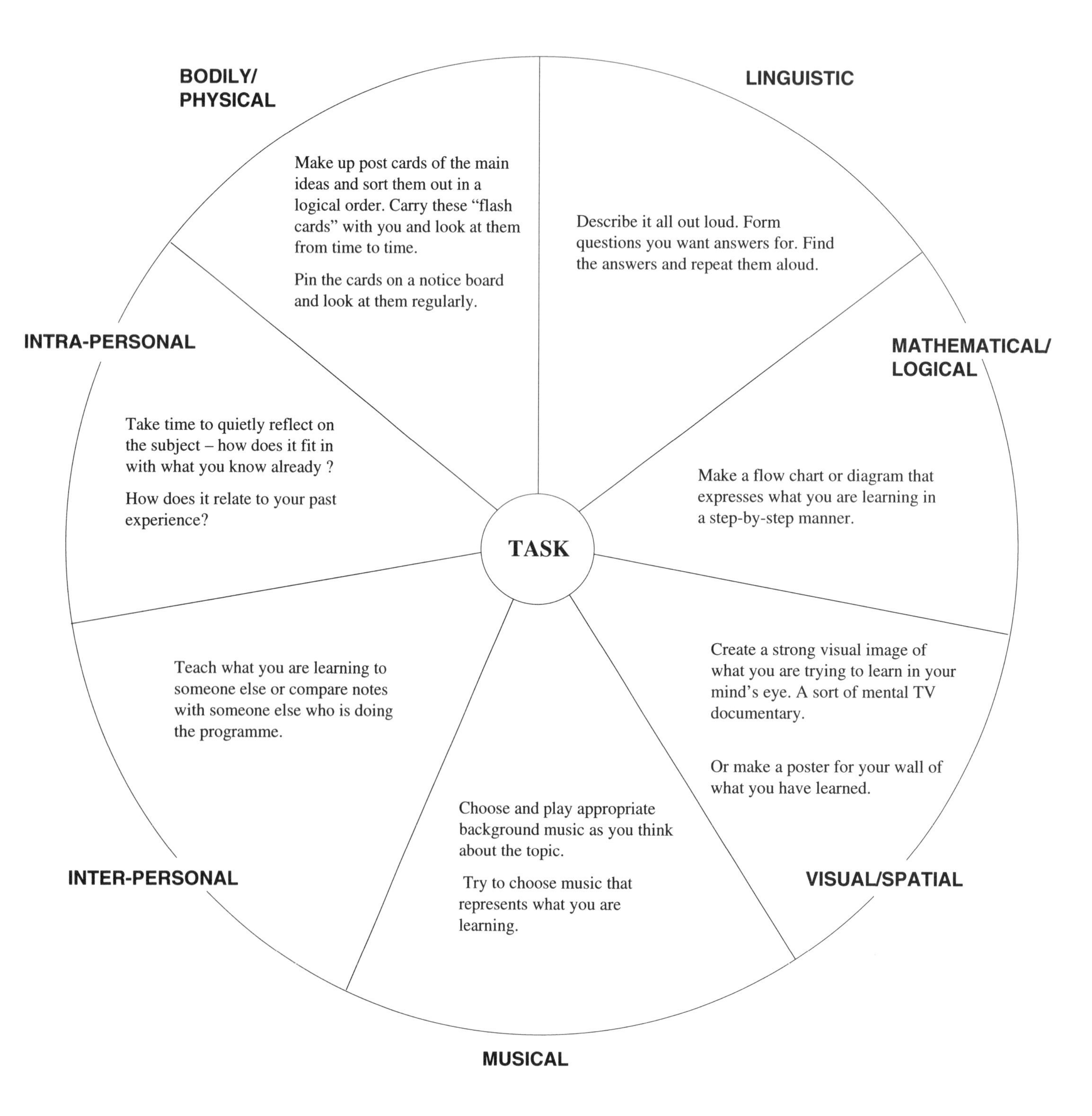

Notes On These Extra Ways To Explore The Subject

Bodily/Physical

When you make notes on cards to pin up or carry with you, you are not only physically engaged in writing, but the handling and sorting of the cards makes the information easier to remember.

In an interesting experiment in Canada, one group of students was given a list of French words to learn. The other group was merely asked to sort the French words out into nouns, verbs and adjectives.

The group who sorted, learned more than the group who deliberately tried to learn! They were having to think about each word in depth to categorise it. They were actively involved.

The simple act of comparing notes with a friend or with colleagues will always surprise you. They will have understood or remembered things you didn't, and vice versa. You also see the ways they approached the task – and you therefore learn about other learning styles.

Musical

Music stimulates the emotional centre of our brain and our emotions are strongly linked to our long term memory. So playing some background music – especially quiet classical music – has proved to be a very effective strategy for many people. (You can read more about this on page 170.)

Intra-Personal

When you are learning anything, a good "strategy" (i.e. useful method) is to find a way to compare what's new with what's familiar.

If you are trying to understand how a carburettor works, for example, it helps to compare it with a perfume spray. The perfume spray sucks up both the liquid and air at the same time. Then it blows both the air and perfume out together in a fine mist.

A carburettor works in a similar way. It sucks up petrol and air together and blows them out in a fine mist. This mixture is then burned to provide energy.

We tried to think of how learning could be compared with an everyday activity. We came up with baking a cake. On the next two pages we have compared the process of baking a cake with the process of learning.

Does it help you visualise the process better? If it does, you have learned something else important. The more real or "concrete" you make something that is new, the better you understand it. Often an everyday comparison is a good way to make it real.

Baking a cake

Learning

Stage 1

First you need to get into the right frame of mind. You are clear why you want the cake and you can visualise a successful end result

Get into the right state of mind

When you are learning, you also need to be in a confident frame of mind and you need to be clear about what benefits the learning will bring. You also need to visualise a successful outcome.

Stage 2

Next you need to assemble all the right ingredients. You often skip read the recipe first, then follow it more slowly.

Get the facts

When you are learning you need to assemble all the facts and information. You also need to skip read quickly to get an overview – the big picture – of what it's all about. Then you proceed bit by bit, sometimes stopping to experiment.

Stage 3

Now comes the most important part. Up to now you've only got the ingredients together. To create a cake you need to **actively** mix those ingredients. The more care and effort you put in at this stage the better the result.

Explore what you are learning

This is the critical stage of learning. It's where you take the new facts and relate them to what you already know. Where you actively think about what it all **means.** Where you look for similarities and differences and connections with things you already know.

This active "churning over" in your mind converts something that might be rather theoretical, into something that really **means** something to you personally.

It's the difference between simply trying to memorise something and truly understanding it. You can only use what you are learning and build on it if you truly **understand** it.

Baking a cake

Learning

Stage 4

You may have actively mixed your cake, but it doesn't become usable until you bake it.

Memorise the key facts

The equivalent of baking is where you really fix something in your mind. You look for a way of "locking it all down", so that a small, simple reminder will bring back all you've learned.

Stage 5

Your cake is well-mixed and baked. But you can't tell how good it is until you test it. You do that by offering it to others, and tasting it yourself.

Show you know

You can't know if you've really learned something till you try it out – put it into practice. Only then will you see whether you have really learned it completely, or whether there are still a few gaps in your understanding.

In this way, testing yourself becomes a vital and useful way of knowing how well you have learned. So any mistakes you make provide useful feedback on what more you need to do. You might be able to improve, not just **what** you learned, but **how** you learned it.

Stage 6

You've baked the cake and tasted it. The final step is to ask yourself whether you could improve on it next time.

In this way, you are not just judging the success of this particular cake, but are learning about the art of cooking in general.

Reflect on it

This is a vital stage of learning. Learning is a continuous process. If we regularly look back on specific learning experiences to **draw conclusions for the future,** we are able to improve the whole **process** of our learning.

Reflecting on the experience and asking yourself what you did well, and what you could do better in the future, allows you to direct and control your own life. Powerful stuff!

Haven't We Repeated Ourselves?

Yes! Some of these ideas were mentioned in the Introductory Booklet and in other places in this text. However, some repetition is an important element in learning.

"An hour's industry will do more to produce cheerfulness and retrieve your affairs than a month's moaning."

Benjamin Franklin

When you learn, a memory trace is laid down in your brain. At first it may be quite a weak trace. It's like creating a path through a jungle. The first time the pathway is ill-defined. With repetition, however, the path becomes well-defined and permanent.

Besides, the first time the idea of "multiple intelligence" was only mentioned. This time you have really explored the subject – **which is the vital stage for effective learning.**

Exploration is the vital stage in effective learning.

Be selective

In any given text book, lecture or training session there are important ideas and less important ideas.(Sad to say, even in this book!)

Get used to rationing your precious attention. A constant question should be, "Is this important?" If it is, give it total focus, and make sure you can summarise it in your own words before you move on.

"Neither A Borrower, Nor A Lender Be"*

Here's a problem that shows the value of some of the tools you've learned.

Alex borrowed 100 Francs from Bobby. Then Alex loaned 35 Francs to Clara and at the same time borrowed 40 Francs from Derek. Derek borrowed 25 Francs from Clara and 10 Francs from Bobby.

If they all met together and repaid their outstanding loans – who has the most and who has the least money?

You already **have** all the strategies to solve the problem.

1. Relax.
2. Break it down.
3. Get the big picture.
4. Visualise it.

1. Relaxation **is** important. At first sight this looks dauntingly complex. But it isn't.

2. Break it down. Let's use symbols, (i.e. letters for names).

3. Get the big picture. What the problem really requires you to do, is to visualise where the money went in the first place, and **what happens when it's returned**. Since this involves movement, it would be a good idea to visualise the problem with arrows.

4. Talk it out as you proceed.

So:

A must return	100	to B	A	→	100	→	B
C must return	35	to A	C	→	35	→	A
A must return	40	to D	A	→	40	→	D
D must return	25	to C	D	→	25	→	C
D must return	10	to B	D	→	10	→	B

Now let's put it on a chart.

*** The quote is from "Hamlet" by William Shakespeare**

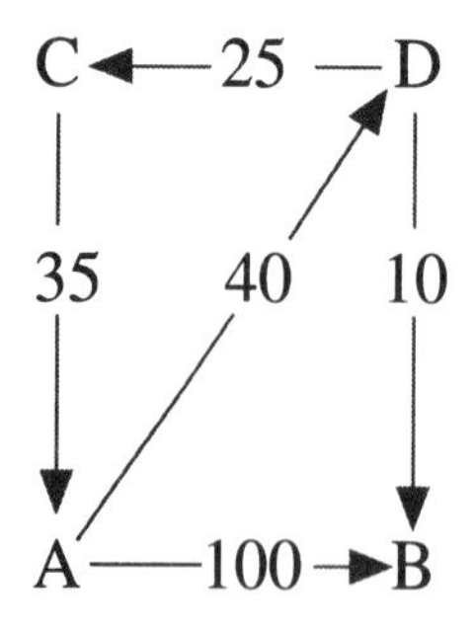

Now the answer is easy.

A has + 35 –40 –100 . . . a total of –105

B has + 100 + 10 . . . a total of +110

C has + 25 –35 . . . a total of –10

D has + 40 –25 –10 . . . a total of +5

So Bobby (B) has the most money and Alex (A) has the least.

The answer was achieved because we were able to find the essential pattern in the problem, break it down into small steps and **visualise** it.

Arthur Whimbey, an expert on learning, says that if you cannot initially solve a particular problem, it's merely that you have not yet had enough experience with that type of problem to see the **pattern** in it. Once you see the pattern, you only need to be systematic and accurate to solve it.

That's why mathematics, for example, is not so much a test of intelligence. It's a test of how well you know the relevant techniques and rules – and how carefully and accurately you apply those techniques and rules. After that it's practice. All these factors are in your control.

Summary

You have been introduced to 14 effective ways to explore the subject in depth. Two for each of the seven intelligences. You can use any combination of these you choose. Typically you might use one or two types of exploration for any given learning task. Which activity you choose will depend on your personal learning preferences – and the task in hand.

Different types of exploration will better suit different learning tasks. That's why the idea of a learning tool kit is so powerful. You can now select the right tool for the job.

Using your range of intelligences as you explore creates a full, balanced learning experience. It also allows opportunities for personal development.

Remember the whole purpose of this stage is to bring information to life – to turn it from surface knowledge to deep understanding. To relate what is new to what you already know. To make comparisons, draw conclusions and make it all usable and meaningful for you personally. That's true learning.

Simply memorising facts may be necessary as a basis for future ideas, but it's not what true learning is about.

DON'T UNDERESTIMATE THE IMPORTANCE OF INDIVIDUALITY

Tests show that simply shifting a book to the left or right of the body can improve some people's reading speed and understanding!

ACTION

You now have seen – and hopefully explored – up to fourteen ways to explore what you are learning.

- Have you tried them out yet?
- How did the activities help?
- Which ones will you use in future?
- What have you concluded about the way you'll tackle learning in future?
- Were you surprised at what you learned about the way you learn?

REMEMBER

It's the learners who take the time (and effort) to **add** this stage, who succeed. If you miss it out, you never rise above passive i.e. ineffective learning. Perish the thought!

A Learning Map Of Stage Three

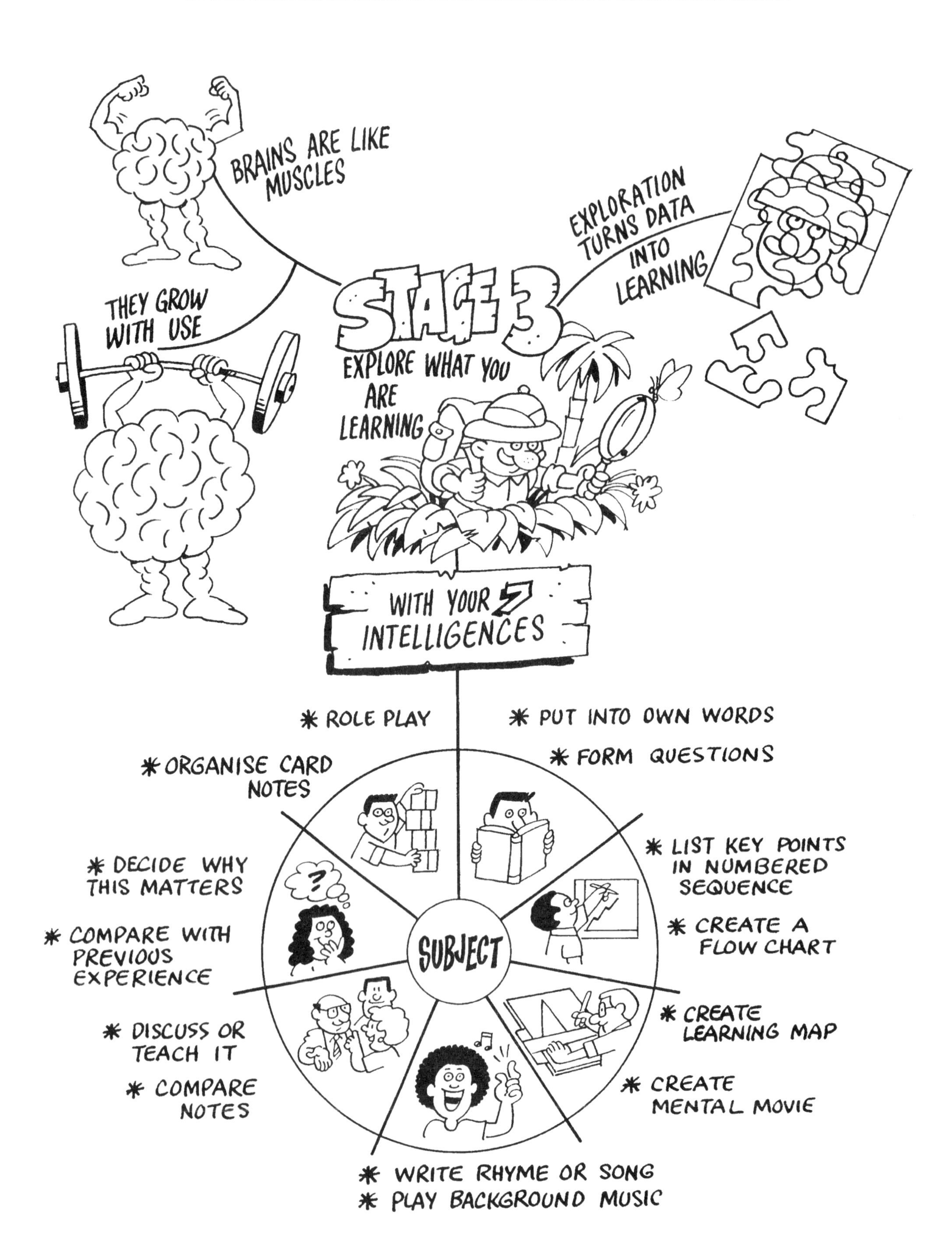

Check what you have learned about Stage Three

1. What is the difference between theoretical data and true knowledge?

2. How many intelligences can you name without checking back in the text?

    1.

    2.

    3.

    4.

    5.

    6.

    7.

3. Is intelligence fixed?

4. What is meant by the "single chance theory of learning"?

5. How can we create Multiple-Chance learning?

6. How do you prevent knowledge from "going in one ear and out the other"?

7. We suggested a total of 14 ways to explore what you are learning. Two for each of the seven intelligences. Can you remember three or four that appeal to you?

Answers on page 215

A time for reflection

If you are a learner at work:

- The main ideas from this section that I will use in my job or career are:

  ____

  ____

- Although I originally did well in my studies, I can see that there are ideas here to learn even better in future. They are:

  ____

  ____

- I didn't achieve everything I could have done at school. But I could start to realise more of my true potential, if I:

  ____

  ____

- The following ideas will enable me to help the people I am responsible for:

  ____

  ____

- As a parent, the ideas that can help my children are:

  ____

  ____

If you are a student:

- The ideas I am going to use to help me learn more effectively are:

  ____

  ____

- Some of the ideas are worth talking over with my friends. They are:

  ____

  ____

- I really feel I would like to discuss some of these ideas with my teacher or tutor. They are:

  ____

  ____

Stage Four

Memorise the key facts

You Can Improve Your Memory

Although it is a bold claim, you will find remembering what you have learned becomes much easier if you learn in the comprehensive stages suggested in *Accelerate Your Learning.*

If you are feeling relaxed and confident about learning, then the parts of your brain that create memories can actually work better. (Stage 1)

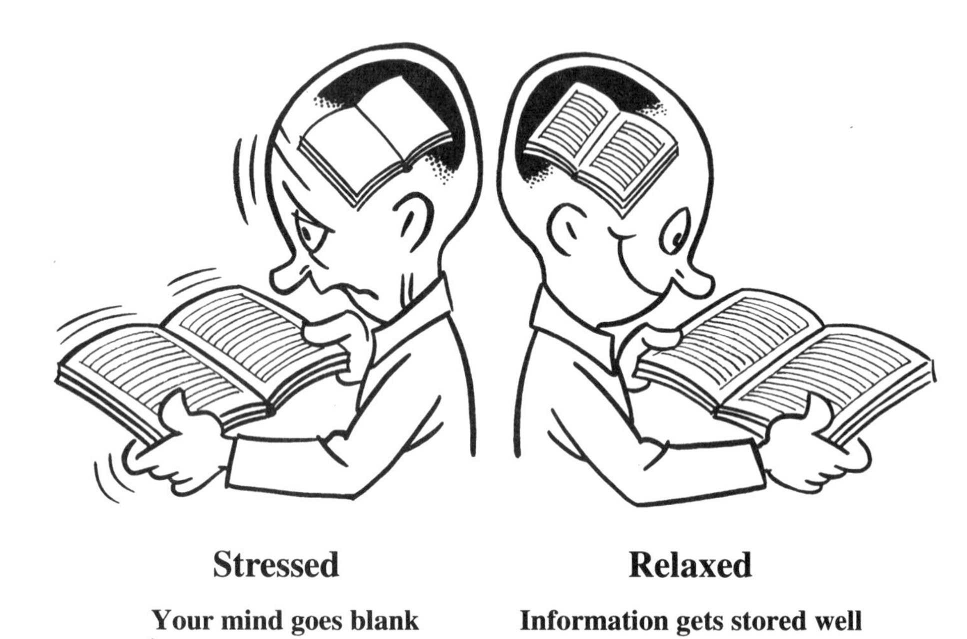

Stressed

Your mind goes blank

Relaxed

Information gets stored well

If you get new information in ways that suit you, then that information is immediately more memorable for you. (Stage 2)

If you explore what you are learning in a variety of ways, then you will understand the meaning of what you are learning. (Stage 3)

Your long-term memory prefers to deal with meanings, so you are feeding your memory with the type of information it likes to work with. Trying to memorise facts without understanding them will achieve little. It's wasted effort.

However, there can still be times when you may need to memorize something such as steps in a process, numbers, spellings or codes. After all, being able to recall certain facts makes our lives easier. It saves time.

You can also pass exams and do your job more effectively if you have essential facts at your fingertips. It's at times like these that some memory tools are useful.

BE VERY SELECTIVE!

The trick is to weed out what is really essential to have at your fingertips. Only try to memorise the key points of the subject.

A Bit About Memory

Obviously there can be no learning without memory. So it pays to know a bit about how your memory works, and how to improve it. Especially as 70% of what you learn today can be forgotten in 24 hours if you do not make a special effort to remember it!

SHORT-TERM MEMORY

. . . is for temporary data.

You have a short-term memory and a long-term memory. Your short-term memory is designed to hold information temporarily. For example, a phone number you have looked up or a sentence someone said. You remember it just long enough to use it.

You can think of your memory like transferring sheep into a big field. Short-term memory is like a holding pen at the entrance to the field. To transfer the sheep into the field, (long-term memory), you need to deliberately drive them in!

If the information is sufficiently important, then it is usually the **meaning** of what you have just learned that is transferred to your long-term memory, rather than the exact words. But you usually need to do something specific to achieve the transfer.

LONG-TERM MEMORY

. . . is for important information.

Researchers have found that information needs to be repeated or acted on in some way in order to be transferred from your short-term to your long-term memory. Exploring what you have learned, using a range of intelligences, is a way to act on it.

Researchers also note that we have separate memories for sounds, sights and feelings. Which is why it makes sense not just to read something, but repeat it out loud and, if practical, find a way to associate it with a physical movement.

For example, if you are learning a foreign language, you would **read** the word or phrase, **speak** it out loud, and **act** it out in an exaggerated way.

It also shows why it is important to make notes as you learn from a talk. You are then listening and writing. So you involve your memory for **sight** (the notes), **sound** (the talk) and **movement** (the physical action of writing).

Your memory is already good!

There's nothing wrong with your memory – you just need to use it properly!

Take a moment and imagine, in your mind's eye, opening your kitchen door. Now, starting with the wall on your left, mentally note down **everything** in your kitchen. The cupboards, the pictures, the kitchen tools, the position of the fridge, oven, cooker, microwave, storage jars etc., etc. Open the cupboards one by one.

The detail you can remember is incredible. And that's just the kitchen. You could do the same with every other room!

Explore how your memory works

Here is a list of words. Relax, then focus on them and read through them **once** slowly. When you have finished, follow the instructions written below the list. You will learn something of importance about your memory!

Grass	Truth	Blue
Paper	Table	Sheep
Cat	Fork	Meaning
Knife	Zulu	Field
Love	Radio	Pencil
Bird	Wisdom	Stream
Tree	Flower	Pen

ACTION

Now cover up the list and write down as many of the words that you recall, in any order.

Now you have finished – and it doesn't matter how many or how few you have remembered – let's see what conclusions we can draw.

If you compare your written list to the full list above, we suspect you will notice the following.

You probably remembered the first words

You tend to remember more of the beginning of any learning session. So you probably recalled "grass", maybe even "paper".

You probably remembered the last words

You also tend to remember more of what you learned at the end of each learning session, so you possibly also recalled "pen", maybe even "stream".

Put these two conclusions together and you have a typical pattern of recall for a learning session as follows:

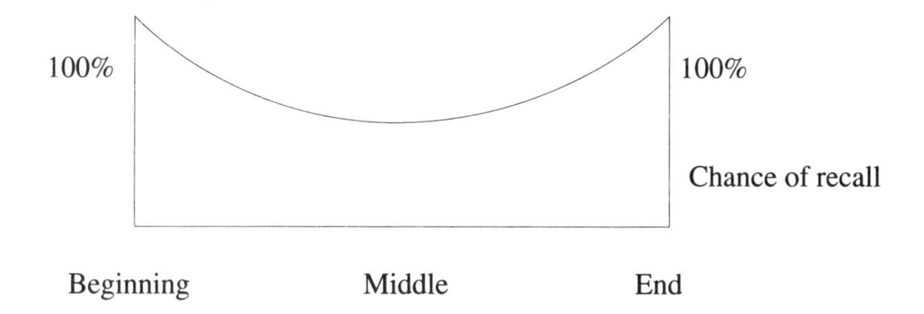

Now here's an interesting "tip". If you want to keep your recall high, have lots of beginnings and endings to your learning session.

The way to do that is to keep taking breaks. Most people find it difficult to really concentrate for more than 20 minutes at a time. So don't force yourself into long learning sessions. Stop frequently and take a "two minute holiday" (use your Motivator Tape).

The effect of taking frequent breaks is to keep your recall level much higher, because you have lots of beginnings and endings!

There is a theory that today's learners are so used to TV presenting information in short "sound bites" and visual clips of two or three minutes, that attention spans have declined.

The media do oversimplify information. That's a reason why we need to learn the tools and techniques to tackle serious books and training sessions properly.

Level of recall

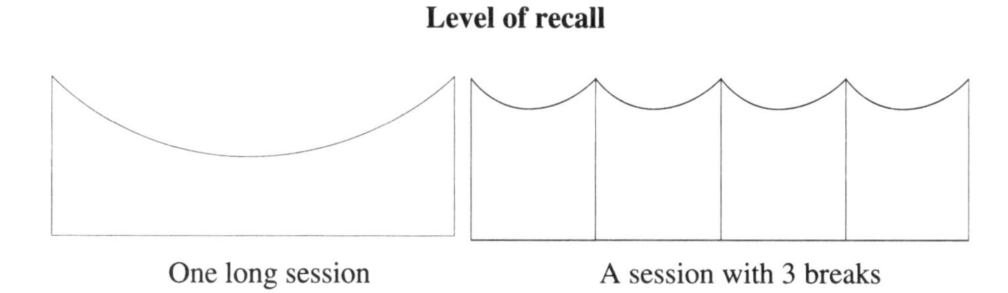

You normally remember what's unusual

You probably remembered the word Zulu. Why? Because it stood out from the list, and it was easy to make a mental picture of it.

We remember what is odd, bizarre, comical or rude! These things are easy to picture in our minds so they are "memorable". If you want to remember something, therefore, try really hard to associate it with a funny or unusual mental image. That is exactly what the professional memory men do, and we will shortly show you how to do the same to remember your car keys or the names of people to whom you are introduced.

You may have also recalled the word "radio" or even "fork" – because they benefited from the extra attention you paid to the word "Zulu". They were next to it, or associated with it.

You remember information that is "organised"

You may have noticed that you automatically wrote down some words in groups. In fact, the list did have certain groups in it. Three groups were:

e.g. **animals –** cat, bird, sheep.

countryside – grass, tree, flower, field, stream.

office – paper, table, pencil, pen.

Organising what you are learning into groups or categories works. The reason is that you are actively doing something with the information, not passively looking at it. You are also forming associations.

You remember "real" things more easily

The list also had words like "love", "truth", "wisdom" and "meaning" in it. These are the least well remembered because they are not specific or concrete. They are not things, they are ideas.

"Real" things are easier to remember than abstract ideas, because you can picture them in your mind's eye. We remember pictures **many** times better than words, so find a way to make a picture of what you are learning, either literally or in your head.

Visual memory is very strong

"A picture", it is said, "is worth a thousand words". The following study from the University of Rochester shows this to be true.

A group of people were shown 2,500 separate photographs – one every 10 seconds!

Three days later they were shown 250 pairs of photographs. The photographs in the pairs were deliberately similar. One picture they had seen, the other picture was new. Yet the respondents could tell, with over 90% accuracy, which of the photos they had seen before, and which they had not.

It is because of the strength of visual memory that we have emphasised so many visual tools of learning: making a mental picture of what is being learned, making a diagram, chart, sketch or cartoon, using colour, highlights and underlining.

When you create your own diagrams or charts you begin to see the pattern in the information. Here's an example. Suppose you were studying the countries in the Far East. Most people have only a hazy idea where they are in relation to each other.

If you draw a simplified picture of the various states, however, you would begin to recognise the area. If you went further and drew the map again from memory, and then compared it with your original copy – you'd really begin to "own" the information.

Can everyone visualise?

At this point some readers will be saying "but I can't visualise".

This concern is based on the misunderstanding that you need to "see" the image, as if it were in glorious colour and cinemascope!

Such vivid visualisation may be extra helpful – but it is not necessary. **Everyone** can visualise sufficiently to improve their memorisation. Here's the proof.

1. **What side of the family car is the steering wheel?**

   The only way you can know the answer is to picture it.

2. **Have you ever worried about anything?**

   Worry is a process whereby you picture something unpleasant and "feel" as if it had already happened. It was not "real", but it felt real. If you can worry – you can visualise!

3. **How many windows in your kitchen?**

   If you know – you can visualise! So, the answer to the question is "yes". Everybody can visualise.

A model of your memory

If you look back at the full list of words on page 148 the chances are that you will recognise that you had originally read all the words.

In other words, your brain had **registered** them, but you could not **recall** all of them. The difference between registration and recall is very important.

In order to recall what you have learned, you need to register it strongly, so it makes an impression. That needs action. The following model, which shows how memory works, helps to define what that action should be.

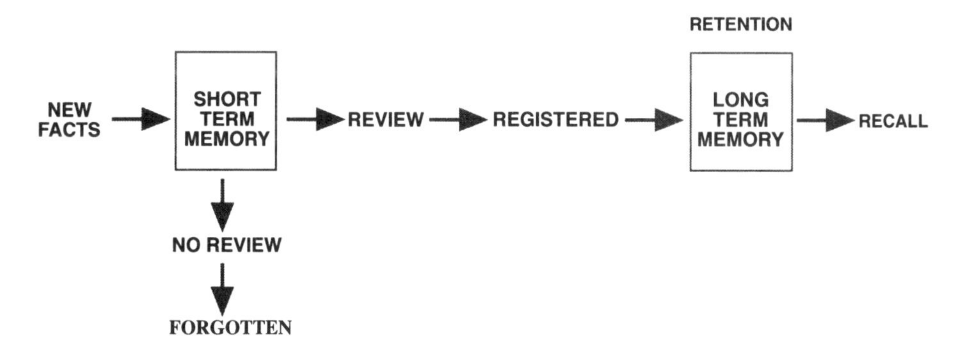

Review – An **active** attempt to remember.

Registration – Getting it into your long-term memory.

Retention – Keeping it there!

Recall – Getting the facts out when you need them.

The four "R's" of memory

If you look at the above model, you will see that if new facts are not reviewed, they simply drop out of the short-term memory. They are forgotten. In one ear and out the other.

What is "review"?

It's an **active** attempt to register information in your long-term memory. You do so by hooking the facts into your visual, auditory and physical memory. The brain has lots of memory sites, and the more sites i.e. (senses) you involve, the better you'll register the new information.

It's like putting reminders up all over your house. The more places to jog your memory, the easier it is to remember.

An ideal time to review what you've learned would be when you go back to the subject after a break. But note that review is **not** the same as simple repetition. Simple repetition, without actively exploring the meaning of the subject, has much less effect.

If you read about something, repeat it out loud, picture it in your head and jot down a couple of reminder words, you've reviewed it visually, auditorily and physically, (the note taking). It is a multi-sensory review.

For this reason the **form** of your rehearsal should vary. Sometimes it can be a re-read of your Learning Maps. Sometimes an out-loud summary. Sometimes a mental "run through", without any notes or prompts at all.

If you want proof of the value of review look no further than a test done on fifteen year olds by researcher Gates. He gave them a list of nonsense syllables to learn. Nonsense words are the most difficult to learn, because they lack meaning.

Here's what he found. Notice the students spent exactly the same length of time on the learning task – it was only the **way** they spent their time that differed.

%of time reading	% of time spent on review	Av. No. of syllables remembered
100%	0%	65
80%	20%	92
60%	40%	98
40%	60%	105
20%	80%	137

Conclusion

Time spent reviewing can at least **double** your recall. Other studies show a **four** times improvement.

People who do not review as they learn are constantly putting new information in, but then allowing that information to slip away. That makes learning difficult, because there will be less data in their brain on which they can hook – or associate – the next lot of new information.

Spending a little time to register something properly at the beginning, saves a huge amount of time later. The simple truth is that most information is not forgotten, it was never shifted from short-term memory into long-term memory in the first place.

A good strategy to ensure you have strongly registered new information is to **deliberately** create links, or connections or associations.

WORTH THINKING ABOUT

One of the reasons we like learning maps is because they allow you to create links between ideas – associations you may not have seen before. And these associations help memory.

Did you notice that Learning Maps look a lot like brain cells? The theme in the middle with ideas branching out from them. Maybe that's why learning maps seem to work the way your brain works?

The Importance Of Making Associations

Think of your memory like a library with thousands of books (i.e. facts) stored in it. If the books were stored in a haphazard manner – or in an irrelevant manner such as by size or colour – then it becomes almost impossible to retrieve any one book. There is no logical connection.

However, if the books are stored in an organised way, (e.g. by subject and author), then retrieval or recall becomes easy and quick.

So to remember well, create plenty of strong connections or associations.

Here are two studies that show the value of **active** linking in creating powerful memories.

Study 1

Three groups of students were each asked to learn 10 new words.

Group 1 just read the words.

Group 2 sorted the words by type of word.

Group 3 formed sentences that contained the words.

Results?

Group 3 remembered two and a half times better than group 1.

Study 2

The students were asked to learn pairs of words. Like Dove + Car.

Group 1 read the words silently.

Group 2 read a sentence aloud that contained the words.

Group 3 made up their own sentence and read it aloud.

Group 4 made a vivid mental picture where the words interacted with each other e.g. the Dove just missed a speeding car.

Which group do you think did the best?

Each Group did better than the one before it, and the final group learned **three times** better than the first.

How might they improve the results even further?

By asking Group 4 to describe, outloud, their mental image of the words interacting. In this way you would have a story with interactive pictures **and** sound.

A story is always a good memory aid because it links words together in a sequence, and because it's easy to picture in your mind.

Example:

You can remember the names of the Seven Dwarfs from this story:

When I woke up this morning at seven o'clock, I felt really DOPEY. I'm not usually SLEEPY in the morning, but this morning I felt GRUMPY.

I wasn't HAPPY, because I had to visit the DOC.

I'm normally quite BASHFUL about going, but the big bunch of flowers had made me SNEEZY, so I simply had to go.

ACTION

Read the story and then read it again aloud.

Then see if you can write down the names of the Seven Dwarfs from memory.

Associations create meaning

We remember things that have a **meaning** for us. And things have meaning when you can connect or associate them with what you already know. When we learn a foreign language, for instance, it's useful to **start** with the points of similarity to our native tongue.

Here's an example. Accelerated Learning Systems Ltd publishes Language Courses. They contain an idea we call "The Name Game". The principle behind the Name Game is that English has evolved from both Old German and Latin. Indeed a few hundred years ago Old German and Old English were very similar languages.

Naturally, over time, German and English began to look and sound different. However, in an hour or so it is possible to uncover many of the underlying similarities between the two languages. In other words to set up the **association** between the languages. Then learning German not only becomes rather an intriguing game, but it's possible to recognise literally **thousands** of words of German after only an hour or two's study. That's a major motivation!

Let's take a brief look at this approach. It's called The Name Game because it's in a question and answer "game" format.

1. If **"malz"** in German = "malt" in English what might you conclude?

   That the **"z"** sound in German has, over the years, sometimes changed into a **"t"** in English.

   If that is true, what do you think the following words mean?

Katze	**Zweig**	**Zu**	**Zinn**	**Zoll**	**Salz**
(cat)	(twig)	(to)	(tin)	(toll or duty)	Salt

2. If "**Bein**" in German = "bone" in English, what might you conclude?

   That sometimes, (obviously not always), an "ei" sound in German has developed into an "o" sound in English.

   So figure out the meaning of:

   Stein, Ein, Eiche (stone) (one) (oak)

   Knowing just the above, it is possible to work out for yourself why **"zwei"** in German means "two" in English.

To continue:

3. "If "**danke** in German is "thank" in English, what might you conclude?

   That "d" in German is sometimes "th" in English.

   So figure out the meaning of:

   Dorn, Ding, Dick (thorn) (thing) (thick)

   This "principle" even works for words that look different. So **"Dach"** = "roof". It makes sense when you realise that roofs used to be **th**atched!

4. In many European languages the "b" sound and "v" sound can easily be transposed.

   So **"Ich habe"** = "I have"

   Armed with this principle you can figure out why **"Ich gebe"** = "I give"

   It even gives you a wonderful insight into why the German word for "to die" = **"sterben"**.

   It doesn't look very similar, until you realise that "to star**v**e" is a specialist form of dying!

HOT TIP

Here's another simple but effective idea for learning foreign languages.

Label the objects around your house with their foreign language names.

You have a constant reminder and an opportunity for subconscious learning.

It is possible to explore this type of approach for almost all the European languages because they have origins in either old German or Latin.

The Name Game makes an effective "entry point" into learning a language for many people because:

1. It creates meaning fast. All of a sudden what looked like a huge learning task begins to shrink down quickly.
2. You see that there is **pattern,** a connection between the languages. That suits the "global" learner, yet it also suits the logical leaner who likes to work out the "rules" involved.
3. It creates a good optimistic frame of mind at the outset. Not only do you get a fast start, but the language is no longer so strange or forbidding.
4. It is rather fun, and you get involved.

   In short, it's "meaningful", and when something has meaning for you, it's easily remembered.

ACTION

Whenever you have something new to learn, ask yourself what connections or associations it has to things with which you are already familiar.

"Sleep on it" is good advice

Often we "forget", because the information was never really registered properly. Sometimes, however, information just seems to fade from your memory. For this reason, early researchers thought that memory gradually faded, rather like a piece of curtain can be faded by the sun.

We now know that memory becomes blurred when new information is so similar to what we already know, that the newer experiences simply "interfere" with our memory of the previous material.

It is, therefore, not predominantly the passing of time that causes memory to fade. It's interference by similar things we have subsequently learned.

You can help combat this process by deliberately interrupting an important learning session by an overnight sleep.

Researcher Chris Evans believed that **the** most important function of sleep is to allow our brain to consider the new things that had been learned during the day. They are then filed and consolidated into our memory system. This happens during Rapid Eye Movement sleep, or REM sleep.

REM sleep occurs when our eyes move rapidly behind our closed lids at night. These REM sessions coincide with dreaming, which led Chris Evans to speculate that we sleep in order to dream. In turn, we dream in order to sort and integrate our new experiences into the existing networks of our memory.

According to this theory, the sleeping brain is like an off-line computer. No new information comes in during sleep, instead the time is taken up with making sense of what we've already experienced or learned.

The implication of this theory is that the ideal pattern would be:

1. Learn.
2. Review the material briefly before sleep.
3. Sleep.
4. Briefly review the previous day's learning again.

Researchers Jenkins and Dallenbach tested this pattern. They asked two groups of students to learn a word list for the same amount of time. Then the first group was tested after eight hours of daytime activity. They scored 9% correct recall! The second group was tested after eight hours sleep. They scored 56% correct recall!

If an intervening sleep isn't practical, a period of different activity, such as listening to music or exercising, will cause less interference and help the process of memory.

The fact that similar material interferes with i.e. weakens memory, would argue for varying your subjects throughout the day. So if you are a student, don't study geometry immediately after algebra. Instead learn something completely different, such as French.

Concentration and the law of predominant attention!

Some professionals like to dress up common sense in fancy names! The law of predominant attention merely means that the mind can only attend to one thing at a time.

You may **think** you can listen to the radio and read a book at the same time. In practice, however, your attention is rapidly shifting backwards and forwards between the book and the radio – inevitably reducing your attention to the book.

Obvious though it may be, to register new information strongly requires that you focus full attention on it. A camera will take a poor picture if the lens isn't focused properly. Similarly your memory will be vague if your senses are not totally focused on the learning task.

Concentration is simply a habit. The more you practice it the easier it becomes. **No-one** concentrates solely on a subject well for more than a minute or so. The people who concentrate (and, therefore, can learn well), have simply practised the habit of bringing their minds back to the subject each time it wanders.

It's the nature of the mind to wander, so initially this degree of concentration will feel unnatural.

If something else is really bothering you, then either deal with it then – or make a note of it and promise yourself you'll deal with it later at a specific time.

It's also an excellent time to use an affirmation such as "This is useful and interests me. I will remember it". Memory is helped by the **intention** to remember.

Putting it all together

This has been a lengthy background on memory. So let us take a moment to summarise how it can help create the conditions for excellent memorisation.

How to remember more from any learning situation

1. First relax, and let go of any concerns. Then take frequent breaks every 20 – 30 minutes.
2. Make any new information memorable by **doing** something to it.
   - Highlight with colour (your emotional middle brain likes colour and takes notice of it).
   - Make an active mental picture of the information. Visualise scenes, words or parts actually moving or draw a picture.
   - Sort the information into groups or lists.
   - Read it aloud. Even read it aloud in a funny accent! (You remember what is unusual or bizarre – so use that fact to your advantage.)
   - Find a connection, an association between what you have just learned and what you already know.
   - Summarise what you have learned out loud, in your own words. This is an absolutely key skill. People who spend some time repeating material, remember at least **twice** as much as people who only spend their time reading and re-reading.

REVIEW HELPS MEMORY

To really become expert at anything requires practice. Knowing something once does not guarantee you'll know it for ever.

Just as sportsmen need constant practice, so you need to keep your learning topped up regularly.

See the review plan on page 166.

Another simple, but highly effective way to "lock down" what you are learning is to keep glancing back at what you have learned. **The more often you review things in your mind, the more firm the impression you will make.**

Remember that jungle path. The more often you walk down it, the more clearly defined is the path. That's why review and repetition helps learning.

Let's now look at how you can improve your memory for three everyday tasks. How to remember people's names, where you left your keys and your personal identity number at your bank's cash point.

How to remember names – and match them to faces

The reason why most people find it difficult to remember names is that people's names rarely have any direct association with their faces. That's because you **hear** the name, but **see** the face.

It was easy in the old days when Mr. Baker baked bread, Mr. Carpenter made furniture and Mr. Thatcher mended roofs.

The secret to remembering names is to create a strong visual association between the name and the face.

Here's how:

- Start by **expecting** to remember. Say to yourself , "**I will remember** this person's name."
- Look thoroughly at the newcomer. Concentrate and take in:

The Hair	It's not just hair. It's long or short, straight or curly, black, blond, brown, grey, etc.
The Eyebrows	They are not just strips of hair. They are arched or thin or bushy or meet in the middle.
The Eyes	They are not just brown or blue. They are large or small, close or wide-set.
The Nose	It's small or large, long or snub, narrow or wide, straight or curved.
The Face	It's round or oval or square.

When you really **look**, rather than glance, you will see an incredible variation in detail.

You have now registered the face strongly.

The next step is to create an association between the visual appearance of the face and the name.

- Repeat the person's name straight away – and explain why you are doing so. Explain you would like to remember the person's name, and that repetition works! If it's relevant, ask the person to spell the name for you.

  People are naturally emotionally attached to their name, and they will be flattered by your interest.

- If you have time, ask if they know the origin of their name. It's a great way to create a stronger association.

- Look for a visual link between the person's face and their name. Something that associates the physical characteristics of their face with their name. If possible, exaggerate the characteristics like cartoonists do, because that makes them more memorable.

- Ask yourself "Who else do I know with the same name?", and try to picture the two people interacting in some way. (You don't ever have to say what you thought of!!)

- Finally, visualise the person's name stamped on their forehead.

When you say good-bye, repeat the name again, and make a decision to recall the place where you first met.

Now read back over this formula for remembering names. What do you conclude?

Many people are disappointed! They expected a"party trick". A magic idea that takes one minute to learn, and requires no effort to do.

Unfortunately, memory (and learning) aren't like that. The "secret" of success is very simple. Learn the skill and make an effort to apply it. It's no different to playing football or riding a bike. You can do it, if you make the effort.

The skill is to:

- Really concentrate hard on the face.
- Find a way to associate or link the name with the face.

THE REASON! 

The real reason we forget names is because we hardly ever try to remember them. We glance at the person, hear the name IN OUR SHORT-TERM MEMORY, but make no effort to actually move it over to our long-term memory.

It is not that we forget the name – it just never entered our long-term memory at all.

Remember that in order to drive those sheep out of the holding pen, you need to ... TAKE ACTION!

How to remember your Personal Identity Number (P.I.N) i.e. cash card number

One of the most useful modern inventions is the wall machine that dishes out cash at your local bank. Pity it doesn't give you a loan!

Here's a great way to remember your P.I.N number instantly and forever.

Say your number is 4285. Simply invent a memorable phrase or sentence that uses a four letter, two letter, eight letter and five letter word. Memorize the phrase and you can always work out the numbcr. Words are easier to remember them numbers because they **mean** something!

A phrase might be "grab my invested money".

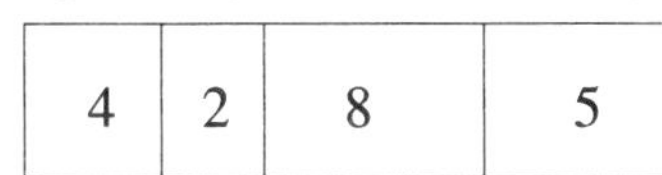

4	2	8	5

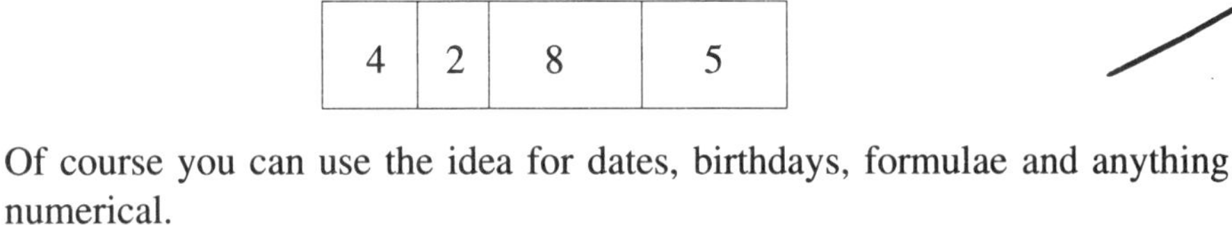

Of course you can use the idea for dates, birthdays, formulae and anything numerical.

How to remember where you put you car keys

It should now be quite easy for you to work out how to remember where you put your keys.

Think of a good way, based on what you have learned.

ACTION

Write down your ideas

____

____

One way is to set them down, deliberately. Then notice exactly in what shape they are lying, what surface they are on, and what they are lying against. Imagine you were going to paint them! (It takes, maybe, 10 seconds.) Then, step away and blink your eyes as if you were photographing them.

Want to be sure to remember something important later in the day?

Switch your watch to your other hand. It's a constant reminder that something is different.

You'll now remember where they are, when you want them. Because now, they haven't dropped out of your short-term memory, they have entered your long-term memory, and are available for recall.

Having a good memory is easy, when you know how! Concentrate, and create as many associations as possible, especially visual ones.

Remembering what you've forgotten

When we forget something, we tend to concentrate on what it is that we have forgotten. But that's illogical reasoning, because we **have** forgotten it!

Instead use the power of association. Retrace in your mind what led up to, and what followed the forgotten event, name, fact, or article. What were you doing, thinking, feeling, saying? Who you were with? What were your physical surroundings?

Think of it like a hole into which the forgotten item has disappeared. You are interested in examining only the surroundings of that hole in great detail. When you have all the associations, say to yourself **positively** "I shall shortly remember". And then leave it to your subconscious. You will usually find that the answer will emerge.

Sometimes it's a help to add another association by slowly going through the alphabet. In most cases you will get a strong feeling for which letter of the alphabet the forgotten item begins with. That triggers the memory.

Memory Demands Action

There are many ways to make sure you remember. Here are some tools for remembering both complex information and for remembering simpler things such as difficult spellings. As with everything you meet in *Accelerate Your Learning* you will need to explore these tools to find out what works for you.

ACTION

Before reading about the ways you can improve your ability to remember, choose three things you would like to memorise. You can choose anything – a simple shopping list, the words of a song, the birthdays of members of your family, a formula, a series of steps in a process.

Then explore the ideas we discuss by using one of them to memorise your choices.

I WANT TO REMEMBER

1 ______________________________

2 ______________________________

3 ______________________________

There are 18 Memory Tools in the next few pages. They are indicated like this.

The reason why witnesses of an accident are so unreliable is that they never intended to remember the scene.

In contrast, a study of blind teenagers showed they had a much better memory for verbal information than sighted children, because they ***intended*** *to remember.*

So – state your intention to remember the words positively, and you will.

Make a decision to remember

The action you have taken above, i.e. writing down three things you want to remember, demonstrates the first and most important step you need to take if you are going to commit something to memory. **Make a definite decision that you are going to remember.**

Learning is more effective in regular, short bursts of about 30 minutes each.

Plan regular breaks

Have you ever sat in a lecture or training session feeling more and more uncomfortable and restless, your attention wandering as time wore on? You will know from such experiences that lengthy working sessions do not lead to good learning.

After 30 minutes maximum you need to take a break. This break should allow you a complete rest from what you are learning. The break need only be 2 – 5 minutes. Try drinking water at each break – our bodies are more than 70% water and a regular glass of water can keep us more alert.

Stretching is an effective break. Reach up above your head and pretend to pick grapes from an overhead branch. It gets air into your lungs and your body is refreshed.

You often can exert more control in a situation than you think. In a training session, it would be reasonable to discuss your need for breaks with a trainer. Many trainers would be impressed that learners would want to take this kind of responsibility for their own learning.

"Review" during and after learning

Throughout *Accelerate Your Learning*, we have constantly asked you to think about what you have just learned, and repeat it in your own words. Repetition is an essential stage in creating long-term memory.

We have also repeated many of the important ideas in different ways. That is deliberate.

You should repeat what you have learned, immediately after first reading about it, and again after exploring it.

It is also important to review what you have learned on a regular basis in the days that follow. This helps long-term memory to form.

You can often review key parts of what you have learned in spare time that would otherwise be wasted – for example waiting for a bus or while you are doing something that doesn't require a lot of concentration.

An example of an effective review plan:

1. Learn the material.
2. Review it briefly after an hour.
3. Review it again after one day.
4. Review it again after one week.
5. Review it again after one month.
6. Review it again after six months.

Each review should take only a very short time – say three to four minutes. And each review should **only** be of the notes you took or the highlighted sections – never the original book. Only go back to the original book if you want to get clear on something.

This pattern of review can lead to very substantial improvements in remembering. In fact studies have shown that instead of forgetting 70% after 24 hours, you can **remember** 80% after six months, with this simple sequence of rehearsal.

So, for an expenditure of perhaps 20-25 minutes, you could almost triple your memory efficiency.

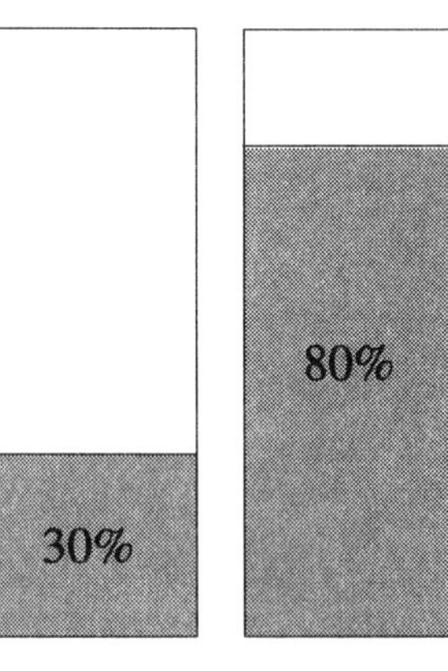

*What you remember after 24 hours **without** a review cycle.*

*What you remember after 6 months **with** regular reviews.*

Create multi-sensory memories

We have learned that we have a separate memory for what we see, what we hear and what we do. Multi-sensory experiences help us to form long-lasting memories.

So, when you want to remember, it will suit you to do everything you can to ensure there is a Visual, Auditory and Physical experience in your learning.

1. **Making notes or a learning map as you learn from a talk**

   You listen (Auditory), make the notes or map (Physical) and see what you have written or drawn (Visual).

2. **Remembering the steps in a process**

   You watch as someone else demonstrates the process (Visual), say out loud the steps in the process, (Auditory), and "walk through" or act out the steps yourself, (Physical) before actually attempting it for real.

Make your own list of the main tools of learning.

Carry it with you and use it when you are in a training class, lecture or are studying.

Plan (visualise) it.

Explain it.

Do it.

3. Make visual images interact

Visual memory is normally the strongest. If you can create not only a visual image of the things you are learning – but make them link together in some way, then you have a powerful memory aid.

Try to picture the image AND the feel or sound of the new subject. Make this as active, **and interactive**, as possible.

We remember things better when they involve:

"I shut my eyes in order to see."

Paul Gamarin

a. **Movement**

Picture a horse standing – and now galloping. Which is the stronger image? Movement adds memorability.

Move the image forwards (or backwards) in your mind. Make things dance together or stand on top of or below or inside one another. You can even add temperature by imaging things as freezing or hot. Make it memorable by making it move.

b. **Humour/Bizarreness**

Funny things are well remembered, so is the unusual and the vulgar!

c. **Colour**

Add colour and brightness to your image.

Detail and movement are the key to a vivid and therefore memorable image.

An example would be visualising the use of the Six Stages of Learning to tackle a text book.

1. See someone in a **relaxed state,** feet up on the settee.
2. See her **getting the facts** with enormous eyes (like an owl), ears (like a bat), and fingers (like a monkey).
3. See her crawling over the book and **exploring** it with a magnifying glass.
4. See her **memorising** the key facts which are stencilled in white on the front of the book which is red.
5. See her **testing** herself out on the key facts, like a quiz show contestant.
6. See her leaning back, **reflecting** on what she learned in a daydream state.

The use of imagery for learning and remembering is **so** powerful that we have included a complete and separate **Super Skill Module** on it. Look especially for the TV Documentary idea.

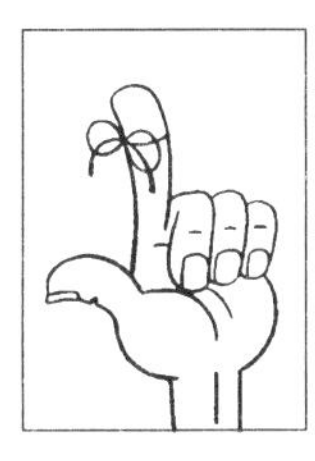

Improve your spelling – instantly!

To remember the spelling of a particular word, simply create a multi-sensory memory of that word in order to firmly establish it in your long-term memory.

1. First "chunk" the word up into syllables.

For example, the word "Psychiatrist" would be split up as ...

PSY – CHI – A – TRIST.

First pronounce the **individual** letters in the first syllable i.e. P-S-Y. Then say the whole syllable i.e. "SY".

Next spell out the second syllable i.e. C-H-I. Then pronounce the second syllable i.e. "KI".

Next the third syllable i.e. A.

Finally spell out the fourth T-R-I-S-T, and then pronounce it i.e. "TRIST".

2. Now visualise the syllables as if they were written on a blackboard in white chalk. Imagine the blackboard is slightly above your eye level. Close your eyes and repeat the individual letters and then the sound of the syllables. Try to see the letters clearly.

3. Now create another strong visual memory by writing the word out in bold letters OR write over the word several times in different colours OR write a word in a way that suggests its meaning e.g. S – E – P – A – R – A – T – E.

4. Create a physical memory by writing the word several times on paper OR in large movements in the air OR with a fibre tip or fountain pen whose texture you enjoy using.

5. Complete the auditory memory by saying and spelling the word out loud as a complete word.

This spelling method works well with adults and children alike.

You will also find it an enjoyable and very effective way to learn how to spell words that typically give trouble.

The fourteen most commonly mis-spelled words in offices are:

Practice (noun) / Practise (verb)

Withhold
Occurred
Benefited

Principal (main matter)
Principle (guiding idea)

Incur
Grievance
Concede
Competent
Calendar
Acquire
Accommodation

Try out the method for any that may have given you trouble!

CORRECT MIS-SPELLINGS

*Keep a list of the words you misspell most frequently. Emphasise **where** you used to make a mistake with capitals e.g.*

Wrong	***Right***
Seperate	*SepArate*
Changable	*ChangEable*
Privelege	*PrivIlege*
Independant	*IndependEnt*
Analise	*AnalYse*
Rythm	*RHythm*
Grammer	*GrammAr*

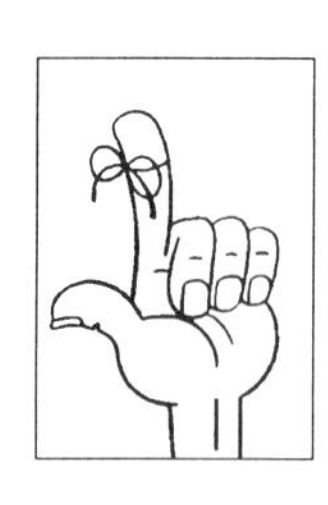

Try a "Review Concert"

You can make what you are learning more memorable by using music as you learn.

This is because:

- Music helps you relax, and you learn more easily when you are relaxed.

- Music stimulates the emotional part of your brain, where an important element of your long-term memory is situated.

- Music makes sure your whole brain is involved in the learning. To oversimplify, your right hemisphere works on the music and your left hemisphere deals with the words.

Music is the universal language of mankind. It creates moods and feelings and pictures without the need for words, so it can be a more direct form of communication than language.

A simple way you can use music is to play a recording that you find appealing, as you review what you want to remember. There are styles of music that are particularly effective for learning, and we have given you some recommendations below.

You can review what you are learning by simply reading a summary out loud as you listen to the music. Another way to do this is to record a summary of what you want to memorise on an audio cassette and listen to it and your music together. Of course you do need two cassette players!

"Music begins where words end."

Goethe

The aim of playing music while reviewing the material is to create what we call a "Review Concert". You sit back quietly, relax and just listen to the words and music. You will be surprised at how it brings back clear memories of what you have learned – like a "Mental Movie". This is a technique that Accelerated Learning Systems uses successfully in its language learning courses.

Accelerated Learning Systems produces a pre-recorded cassette tape of ideal Concert Review Music. It is available from the address at the end of this Manual.

Music that is suitable for a review concert includes

Mozart	Concerto #21 in C major, K467.
Beethoven	Piano Concerto #5 in E flat.
Vivaldi	Flute Concerto #3 in D major.
Bach	Concerto in D minor for 2 violins.
Mozart	Clarinet concerto in A major.
Pachelbel	"Canon" from Canon and Gigue.

Organise material meaningfully

Another way to make what you are learning memorable is to organise or sort what you are learning into groups or categories that relate to each other. In other words, each group contains items that have some similarity to each other.

Now label each group with a key word that in some way expresses the similarity or relationship between the items.

There is an example of how to "organise" material into groups on page 150.

Once you have each group with its title or label you need only memorise the key words. Later, when you recall the key words, you will find you will also be able to remember the items that made up the group.

Learning or Memory Maps are a particularly effective way to do this. They lead you to organise what you are learning on the basis of meaning.

You group ideas together that relate closely to one another and use key words and images to label these groups of related ideas.

You end up with a concise, organised, meaningful, visual and therefore MEMORABLE summary of what you are learning.

For example, a history course can be re-ordered into any number of sub-groups e.g. economic problems, religious issues, domestic conflicts, foreign wars, biographical details, etc. Not only does this produce a degree of novelty, but it helps you see the connections and links between events.

The Six Stages of Learning is a good example of how you can organise a lot of complicated ideas into simple groups or categories.

*Remember the Six Stages and you start remembering the ideas you learned **within** those stages.*

"Memory Flashing"

This exotically named way to remember is **extremely** powerful and simple.

"Memory Flashing" is a very powerful way to embed knowledge.

1. Take your notes in learning map or brief list form
2. Study them carefully for one or two minutes
3. Then set your notes aside and recreate them from memory
4. Now compare the two learning maps or two sets of notes. (i.e. the original and the one you just made). You will immediately see anything you missed out
5. Now make a third set of notes or Learning Map. Again compare your new set of notes or Learning Map with the original.

Create initial Learning Map

Recreate it from memory

Compare the two. The mind instantly focuses on what was missed.

When the original and your new set of notes are the same, you will have created a **very** strong memory for your notes.

Moreover, because a Learning Map is itself a way of concentrating a lot of information into a few brief notes, you may well have recorded a whole book or programme in one easily remembered form. The KEY words will trigger your memory for lots of other detail.

Try this out for yourself at the end of this course. Prepare a learning map that summarises the entire programme. Then use the Memory Flashing technique to really store it away permanently.

Result? You could remember **all** the learn-to-learn techniques with one page of notes!

"Flash Cards"

Try holding flash cards above eye level. Some people find it helps them memorise better.

Some subjects lend themselves to writing on flash cards. Scientific formulae, for example, or foreign words.

You can make use of spare time – travelling on a train or bus for example – by reviewing the flash cards and testing yourself.

Alternatively, get into the habit of carrying a portable note book and noting down key facts in it for regular review.

Flash maps

Flash maps are grown up versions of flash cards!

All you do is create a ring binder for all your learning maps, with dividers in between the subjects. Then file a **copy** of all your learning maps in this binder. In one single document you have a portable personal reference book on your **whole** area of study. I kept a complete 3 year course in such a binder.

The great benefit is that you can revise enormous amounts of material during times that would otherwise be wasted. It's a powerful idea with only one vital warning. It's wise to make a copy of each Learning Map, and put your name and address on the folder. You would not be thrilled to leave three years' work on a bus!

A well-known mnemonic is "Richard Of York Gave Battle In Vain". It reminds you of the colours of the spectrum.

Red, Orange, Yellow, Green, Blue, Indigo, Violet.

Invent a Mnemonic!

A mnemonic (pronounced nem – on – ic) is just a fancy name for a memory aid.

One of the most common – and useful – is an acronym. An acronym is a word made up from the first letters of what you are trying to remember. A well-known acronym is N.A.S.A. – standing for National Aeronautical Space Agency. Another one is SCUBA (as in scuba diving). It stands for Self Contained Underwater Breathing Apparatus.

You can make this type of memory aid into a single word – or a sentence. Musical students remember notes and their place on the stave with the sentence "Every Good Boy Deserves Fun" and the word "Face".

E F G A B C D E F

Why not try to make up a mnemonic for the Six Stages of Learning yourself?

Mnemonics are good for memorising chemicals. Many chemicals are known by letters – Potassium is K, Sodium is Na, Iron is Fe, Copper is Cu etc.

For example:

***K**een **Au**nt **Ag**atha **Ca**n **Cu**t **Al**l **F**elicity's **Na**ils.*

This represents:
Potassium, Gold, Silver, Calcium, Copper, Aluminium, Iron and Sodium.

*Finding creative symbols for your **own** mnemonics is part of the learning process. Once you have produced a mnemonic you will often find that you have already learned it without trying.*

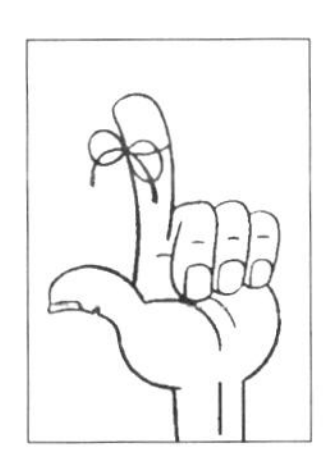

Let it sink in overnight

If you review your notes on a subject for a few moments before getting ready for bed, your learning will benefit.

The brain appears to use sleep as a time to "file away" information and there is a theory that dreams help us connect what's new, to what we already know.

Number the points to remember

This simple idea is one of the most useful. If you number the points, ideas or actions you need to remember, then you will automatically know if you have forgotten one!

That's why we keep talking of the Six Stages of Learning. As you mentally tick off the stages, it also reminds you that there are specific tools to accomplish each stage successfully.

Whole learning

There are times when you need to memorise a lot of material by heart. Perhaps a poem or play. Here's the method. **Don't** learn it bit by bit, line by line – learn it as a whole.

1. Read it all the way through thoroughly, making sure you **understand** it. Go back on any parts that were difficult to understand, and make sure you figure them out. You won't easily remember what you don't understand!

2. Re-read it again quite quickly. And again.

3. Re-read it again, aloud but now **hear** the words in your mind.

4. Re-read it again aloud with as many visual pictures as you can produce. Imagine everything as clearly as possible.

5. Re-read it again aloud, and add actions or movement, as far as is appropriate.

6. Repeat this whole pattern again from stage 1 to 5.

   Certainly that's a lot of repetition, but it's been proven that this "whole to part" method is at least 50% faster than the "part to the whole" method.

   Can you see why?

   It's multi-sensory, and it starts with the big picture or whole pattern.

   Try it – it works.

Over-learning

The literature on memory supports the fact that if you really want to remember something you should "over-learn" it.

In other words, for a really crucial piece of information you should not only review it till you "know it cold" – but even continue to learn it beyond that point. Such information is literally never forgotten because it becomes part of your physical memory.

There is good practical proof of this. Experience tells us that a learning activity like riding a bicycle is never forgotten. We repeat the actions often enough to acquire the skill as a life-long memory.

Chunk it

Here is a way of compressing lots of information into an easily recalled format.

1. Make your notes in a Learning Map form.
2. Title each Learning Map with a **single word**.
3. Invent a mnemonic which enables you to remember all the title words.

For example, there are six Learning Maps that summarise the six stages of learning we have identified. Invent your own mnemonic to remember these six stages, then practice memory flashing to really learn the contents of the six Learning Maps.

Result? You have effectively learned the contents of this whole 200+ page book in maybe an hour of effort.

In turn you will therefore have all the proven tools of learning at your disposal.

The only memory trick we like

Do you remember the way to remember your cash card number? You used words to represent figures. You can extend this idea to memorise dates or figures.

For example:

1616 The year of Shakespeare's death.

Generally with years you can afford to drop the one thousand – since it's obvious. So you want three relevant or funny words. They need to be a six letter word, a one letter word and a six letter word – representing 616. How about . . .

Writer A Genius?
6 1 6

An easier way to remember the start of the French Revolution would be 7/8/9.

Always use the easiest mnemonic.

186,282 miles per second. The speed of light.

How about . . . "A dazzling sunray is flashing by"
1 8 6 2 8 2

1789 The start of the French Revolution.

How about . . . Freedom Democrat Rebellion?
7 8 9

1588 The Spanish Armada.

How about . . . Ships Invading Suddenly
5 8 8

Memorising several definitions

This method works because you have created a memory chain.

Here's the most effective way to memorise a list of, say, twelve key definitions.

1. Memorise the first definition.
2. Memorise the second.
3. Repeat the first and second from memory until you have them absolutely right.
4. Memorise the third.
5. Repeat the first, second and third.
6. Memorise the fourth
7. Repeat the first, second third and fourth etc.

Time Lines

Ask someone to recall an event in the past and their eyes are likely to flick up and to the left as they search their memory. Ask them to imagine the future and the chances are that their eyes will move to the right.

Normally, most dates are listed down the page, and that is not as easy or as natural a way to organise the information for recall.

We tend to visualise time travelling from left to right. It therefore makes sense to organise a sequence of historical dates in the same way, e.g.:

1789	1854	1871	1929	1969
French Revolution	Crimean War	Unification of Germany	Wall Street Crash	1st man on moon

Flow Charts and "clock" patterns

If you want to visualise a sequence of actions for recall, a simple flow chart works well.

Here's a flow chart of the Six Stages of Learning.

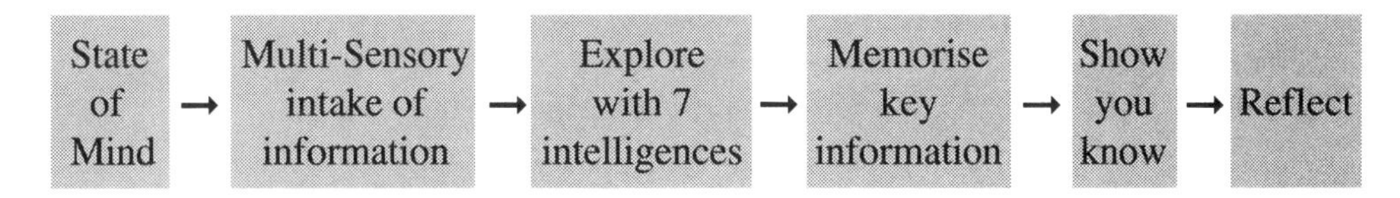

A "clock" pattern can also work well to recall a sequence.

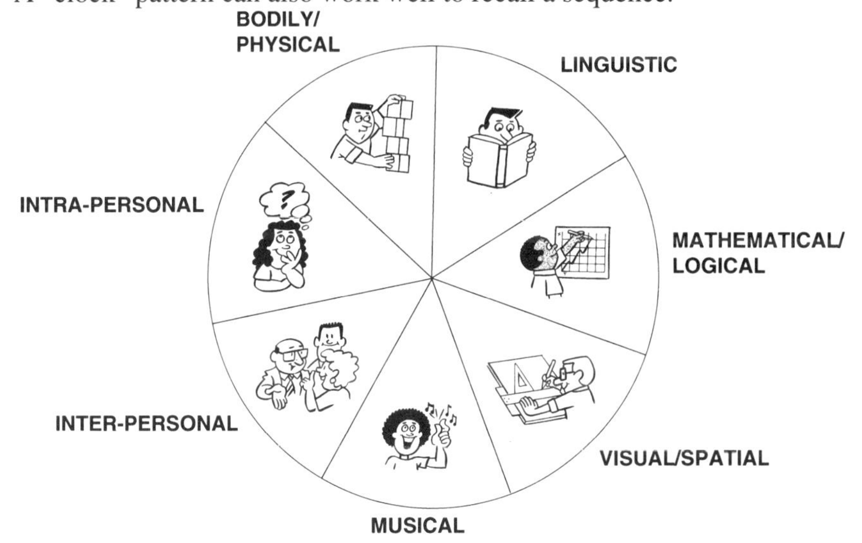

Summary

If you want to make sure you remember what you are learning, then follow through these **"HOT TIPS FOR SUCCESSFUL REMEMBERING".**

1. **Make a firm intention to remember.**

2. **Plan a series of short learning sessions with frequent short breaks.**

3. **Make the information memorable for yourself by:**

   - Creating a multi-sensory memory of it.
   - Making and using flash cards.
   - Memory flashing.
   - Creating memorable associations. ("What does this remind me of?")
   - Organising the material in a logical way.
   - Making up a mnemonic.
   - Numbering the points.

4. **"Lock down" the knowledge by repeating a summary of it over a background of music.**

5. **Review what you have learned:**

   a. After one hour.

   b. The next day.

   c. The next week.

   d. The next month.

   e. After six months.

It helps if you write down your own memory plan and pin it up somewhere you will see it, and therefore remember to act on it.

ACTION

Explore the different tools of remembering and find out what works for you.

Check what you have learned about Stage Four

1. How do you move information from your short to your long-term memory?

2. Why should you take frequent breaks?

3. How does review help you remember?

4. What is the first memory tool?

5. Do we have a separate memory for what we see, hear, say and do?

6. What is memory flashing?

7. How can you improve your spelling?

Answers on page 216

A Learning Map Of Stage Four

A time for reflection

If you are a learner at work:

- The main ideas from this section that I will use in my job or career are:

  ____

  ____

- Although I originally did well in my studies, I can see that there are ideas here to learn even better in future. They are:

  ____

  ____

- I didn't achieve everything I could have done at school. But I could start to realise more of my true potential, if I:

  ____

  ____

- The following ideas will enable me to help the people I am responsible for:

  ____

  ____

- As a parent, the ideas that can help my children are:

  ____

  ____

If you are a student:

- The ideas I am going to use to help me learn more effectively are:

  ____

  ____

- Some of the ideas are worth talking over with my friends. They are:

  ____

  ____

- I really feel I would like to discuss some of these ideas with my teacher or tutor. They are:

  ____

  ____

Stage Five

Show you know

Show You Know

Test, practise and use what you have learned

You have now worked through the first four stages of learning.

Researchers have found that if an idea or skill is used within 24 hours of seeing it or hearing about it, it is more likely to be remembered and used in future.

You've got yourself relaxed, confident and ready for learning (Stage 1).

You've got the facts in ways that suit you (Stage 2).

You've explored what you are learning, using a range of your intelligences, and have therefore understood it properly (Stage 3).

You've made a deliberate effort to remember what you've learned (Stage 4).

You now need to be able to **demonstrate** you have learned, that you have really **understood** the subject, and that you can put it into practice. You must "show you know".

In other words, now's the time to **test, practise** and **use** what you have learned.

How do you know you know till you try?

Three ways to "Show you know"

Nobody ever became an expert overnight. However, you can become an expert by taking three steps to "Show you Know".

1. **Test** yourself to check you've got it.
2. **Practise** to become confident and fluent.
3. **Use** it to make it a part of you.

Often steps two and three can, and do, get combined. We can practise what we've learned by immediately putting it to use. For some people, however, practice is a much needed intermediate stepping stone, as it builds confidence for real life use of new skills.

A test is a chance to explore the limits of what you can currently do or understand. It's an opportunity not a threat.

1 - Test yourself

Whatever we are learning, there is a point where we are a beginner. At this point testing is very important. You need to make sure that you know or can do what you have set out to learn.

Testing yourself should be a straightforward check on your ability to do what you have been learning. Don't worry about doing it quickly or effortlessly. Quite simply, just check whether you've 'got it'.

This is where the learning tools you have already assembled can come into their own.If it's information you are learning, try going over your memory maps or notes. Try Memory Flashing!

"Until you try, you don't know what you can't do!"

Henry James

Test yourself with flash cards. Create a "mental movie" of what you have learned. Do you remember it all? Recreate a flow chart. Try teaching or explaining it to someone else. Create a logical, numbered list. Repeat it out loud in your own words.

Do you see now how useful the learning tools are? They can be used for exploring, memorising **and** testing your learning.

Learning a language

Flash cards not only help you to learn new vocabulary, they are also an excellent way to test yourself.

Write the English word on one side of the card and use the other side for the language you are learning.

Learning to maintain a car

Test yourself by drawing a flow chart of the proper sequence. Also redraw important diagrams you have studied in a manual.

Test yourself on *Accelerate Your Learning*

You may have noticed that we have been prompting you to test yourself throughout this programme. That's why there are questions at the end of each stage. Questions and answers are only one way to test yourself. We suggested others earlier in this section.

ACTION

Test yourself now – name each of the six stages of learning and note some tools that you could use at each stage.

Errors can be useful!

When you make testing yourself an automatic part of the process of learning, you can become more matter-of-fact about mistakes. You come to see the role of mistakes, rather than fear them. Mistakes become an enevitable part of learning.

Any errors you make are helpful feedback about how you are getting on. They clarify any areas of doubt or inability. They tell you where you will have to spend a bit more time – or what you might need to explore more deeply. So an error that you learn from is a sign of progress.

"Mistakes are the staging posts on the road to success."

MISTAKES

The person who does not make mistakes, does not make anything!

Too often we feel that errors reflect on us as individuals, and they affect our self-esteem.

That's wrong. An error should be seen as separate from the person who makes it.

If you do something incorrectly, this does not mean that ***you*** *are a failure. It simply means that you have not* ***yet*** *found the correct way to do it.*

For a parent to say "Bad boy" confuses the person with the deed.

If you disagree with a child on an issue, address the issue rather than criticising them as a person.

Rather than: "You are a bad boy for leaving your room untidy", a more appropriate response might be: "The state of your room at the moment is not what I would expect of you".

Mistakes – it's what type, not how many!

Mistakes represent a chance to see what needs more attention. So concentrate, not on how many mistakes you may have made, but on what **type** of mistakes they are.

For example, a maths student who initially felt depressed at 39 mistakes out of 100 attempts came to realise that he was really making the same type of mistake over and over again. He corrected the misunderstanding that led to the errors, and started producing fault-free work.

"The turtle only makes progress when his neck is stuck out."

Rollo May

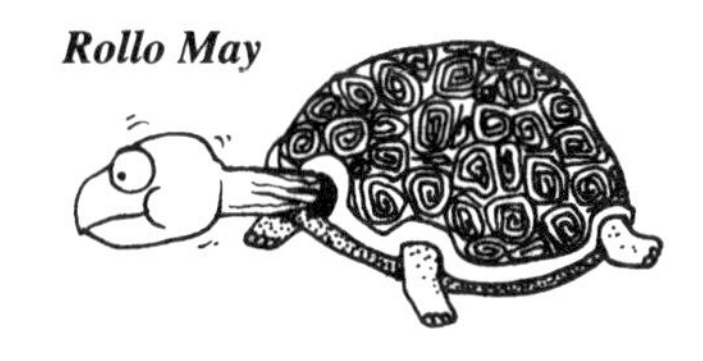

2 - Practise what you've learned

Moving from being a beginner to becoming more expert depends on practice. The typical comment made about experts is "she makes it look so easy". This is because the expert has it all at her fingertips. This easy confidence comes from familiarity through practice.

Whatever you are learning, simple or complex, you need to spend some time to practise the knowledge or skill. Some learners can move immediately into a real life situation. They are happy to practise at work. For others, advance practice helps them to feel really confident that they know the subject.

PRACTICAL PRACTICE

Write out each of the tools for learning you intend to use. One on each card. Then lay out each card in a separate place where you work or study.

Or in a diary, one per day.

Or pin them to the wall.

Or carry them with you.

Practise each technique ***one at a time*** *until it becomes a habit.*

Mental rehearsal and role play

The following are two excellent ways to practise something before you use it in real life. They help you build confidence, foresee possible stumbling blocks and plan how you will deal with them.

Mental rehearsal involves using your imagination to see yourself actually using what you have learned.

Build up a full and detailed picture of yourself in a real life situation and then see yourself, in your mind's eye, performing well. This is a great way to build self-confidence and will actually improve your performance in reality. It is a method used with great success by top class sportsmen.

Top sportsmen all regularly practise in their "mind's eye".

Role play involves either acting out what you have learned alone or with someone else. If what you are going to tackle involves other people, it is a very effective way to practise how you will go about it. You can hear and check out what you are going to say.

Role play gives you a further chance to improve or refine your skills before you use them for real. Again it is a good confidence builder.

Examples of role play and mental rehearsal

Learning a language

Imagine a situation in which you want to be able to use the language you are learning. Practice the conversation you would have – aloud – using gestures and body language.

Learning to maintain a car

Use your imagination and go through an important sequence – for example, how you would change a spark plug. Make the detail really vivid in your mental rehearsal.

Practise the learning tools in *Accelerate Your Learning*

Select a learning tool from *Accelerate Your Learning* – one that you would like to be able to use easily. Work out a practice plan and follow it through.

For example, you would like to be able to use Learning Maps at school, in a training session or at night school, but don't feel ready. Practise by making Learning Maps from television programmes.

"Practice doesn't make perfect. Perfect practice makes perfect!"

Vince Lombardi

You are your own best judge!

One of the things that happens with "formal" learning is that we get used to other people judging us – marking our work! However, it's obviously more satisfying when we become the quality judges of our own work.

"Every job is a self-portrait of the person who did it."

That's why the stage of "show you know" is so important. You set your **own** standards and you check your own performance against them.

If you are a student, get into the habit of looking at your own work before you hand it in. What grade would **you** give it? Is it up to your own best standards? When you get it back, ask what you could have done to get the grade you wanted.

That way your teacher works for you – instead of vica versa.

3 - Use it

INSTINCTIVE COMPETENCE

To start with, you have to "think about" riding a bike. You have to concentrate on what you are doing – it feels awkward – and you fall off a lot!

Gradually, as you practise, it becomes an unconscious skill.

You no longer need to think about it. You just do it instinctively.

Practise the tools of this programme and they will gradually become "second nature". Then you'll find learning is fast, easy and fun.

You really have succeeded when you can use what you have learned independently and away from the situation where you first learned it. That's why this final step in "Show you Know" is essential. Using what you have learned in different ways and for different purposes, developing and improving on it and making it really part of you is true mastery.

It's one thing to learn to use a computer on a course, but quite another to try using that learning in the work place – when perhaps you don't feel too sure of yourself. And yet another level of challenge to explain it to someone else.

If you are a driver, can you remember how you felt the first time you took the car out on the road alone after passing your test? It's that kind of courage that is needed when you transfer something you have learned into real life. To use what you have learned usually means you take a few risks.

Use it within 24 hours

If an idea is used within 24 hours of seeing or hearing about it, it is much more likely to be used permanently. So, if you want what you have learned to stick, use it straight away.

Take every opportunity to practise your new skill!

Look for other examples

Watch other people and take careful note of how they use the skills you are learning. Look at the different settings and circumstances in which they put them to use.

Ask them to explain how they do it. Informal teaching of this sort allows you to see and hear a different view on what you are learning.

Research shows that when you learn from more than one person, you are more able to use the skill in different situations.

Prompt yourself to use it

It's not automatic to remember to use a new skill. So put up some reminders to yourself. A simple note stuck on a fridge or notice board. A hand-out from a training session stuck in a prominent place. Or make yourself a book mark with the learning tools on it, that work best for you.

Getting support from others

Learn with your family

Make a real attempt to involve your family in your learning. If you let them help – for example, by asking them to listen while you explain what you have learned, they are also likely to gain from it.

A family that is involved and understands what it is you are trying to achieve, is less likely to feel resentment about the time you need to devote to learning.

Study Buddies

Find yourself a learning partner – somebody who is also trying to understand and use what you are learning. You can offer each other support as you explore the subject and you can regularly quiz each other to check how you are doing.

Study buddies help, not only by testing each other, but by allowing the partners to compare their approaches. In that way, you get an idea of your progress.

There's another big advantage of the study buddy system – or co-operative learning. It is informal team work. To be able to work easily and well in teams is a skill that all modern organisations value highly.

Learning Circles

Learning circles are groups of people who are tackling the same subject, getting together informally to share their experiences, questions and findings. It is a very effective idea, and it also works very well for foreign languages in organisations.

We think that Co-operative Learning is so powerful that there's a whole section on it in the Super Skills supplement.

Mentors

Find yourself a mentor. A mentor is someone who is highly skilled in the area you are learning about, and who would be encouraging, supportive and a source of further information for you.

A mentor should be somebody with whom you can feel comfortable and who can offer positive feedback, constructive criticism and ideas to try. **You can also learn from his or her mistakes!**

Taking advice is a skill!

"Advice is like snow: the softer it falls, the longer it dwells upon and the deeper it sinks into the mind."

Samuel Tayler Coleridge

It's a pity that we normally grow up regarding advice as something that always comes "from the top downwards". Our teachers give us advice, our boss gives advice. Often it is something that is imposed on us. We rarely ask for it.

Yet the relationship between teacher and student, trainer and trainee or worker and boss **should** be viewed more as a partnership – which, in fact, it is. You would then be more willing to seek advice actively.

If you fail to seek advice from the people around you, you are cutting yourself off from a major source of information, learning and self-advancement.

Here's some advice about advice!

- Ask for it frequently – people **like** to give it. It's flattering.
- Keep an open mind. Experts are good at giving accurate **factual** information. Many are less good at giving judgements. Make a note of those people whose advice seems consistently helpful.
- Avoid being defensive. Sometimes advice is constructively critical. Someone can criticise your actions and work, without criticising you personally. Make the distinction between the two!

"Ignorance produces mistakes, but mistakes produce learning".

F is for Feedback – not Failure!

It is not important always to be right – what is important is to treat each mistake as an opportunity to learn. If the fruit of the tree is out on a limb – you are bound to fall off quite regularly! Progress means taking risks, and risks inevitably lead to some failures. The important point is that they are only temporary!

The whole process of evolution is based on feedback. Over the last 100 years, hedgehogs in England have evolved longer legs. Why? Because as traffic on the roads became heavier they had to run across the road faster!

The hedgehogs with the longest legs survived, bred and passed on those characteristics. The hedgehogs, which did not "learn" from this dramatic form of feedback, did not survive.

A learning log or record

I have a friend who is acquiring a PhD from a leading U.S. University. Yet she didn't speak before she was five and her teachers despaired of her in primary school. She was diagnosed dyslexic.

Her father rescued her faltering academic progress. Every evening, without fail, he would ask her to tell him what she had learned that day "Write down, or draw out on a scroll, what you think were the most important things you learned today".

This not only ensured that she mentally rehearsed what she had learned – she also had a daily record of it. At the end of each week she could look back and **see** her progress. It made it tangible.

A learning log need only include a few brief details – foreign words you've mastered, or a concept you've now grasped, or a computer code you now understand. The point is, it's there in black and white. It's a record of achievement.

You can also use it to jot down a word you heard, but don't know the meaning of. Then you won't forget to look it up later.

You can use the learning log to jot down a question that struck you for which you need to find the answer.

I suggest you experiment with a "learning log". I won't claim it was the only reason that turned my friend from being categorised as someone who was disabled as a learner to someone who gained a PhD – but it certainly was a factor.

Sensing progress is critical. It is true that the longest journey starts with a single step. But few people stay motivated unless they can look back and see how many steps they have already taken!

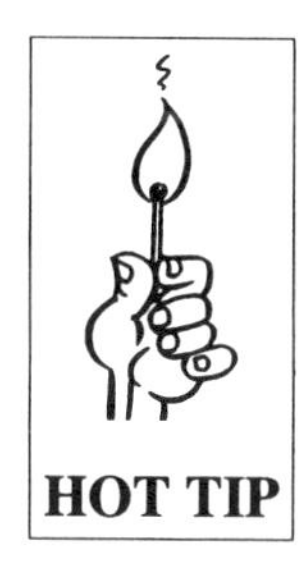

Set up a file into which you can put pieces of work you are proud of or qualifications or records of achievement.

The file will be your own record of achievement.

It grows as you grow in stature as a learner.

It reminds you that learning is a lifelong activity. We never stop progressing.

A Learning Map Of Stage Five

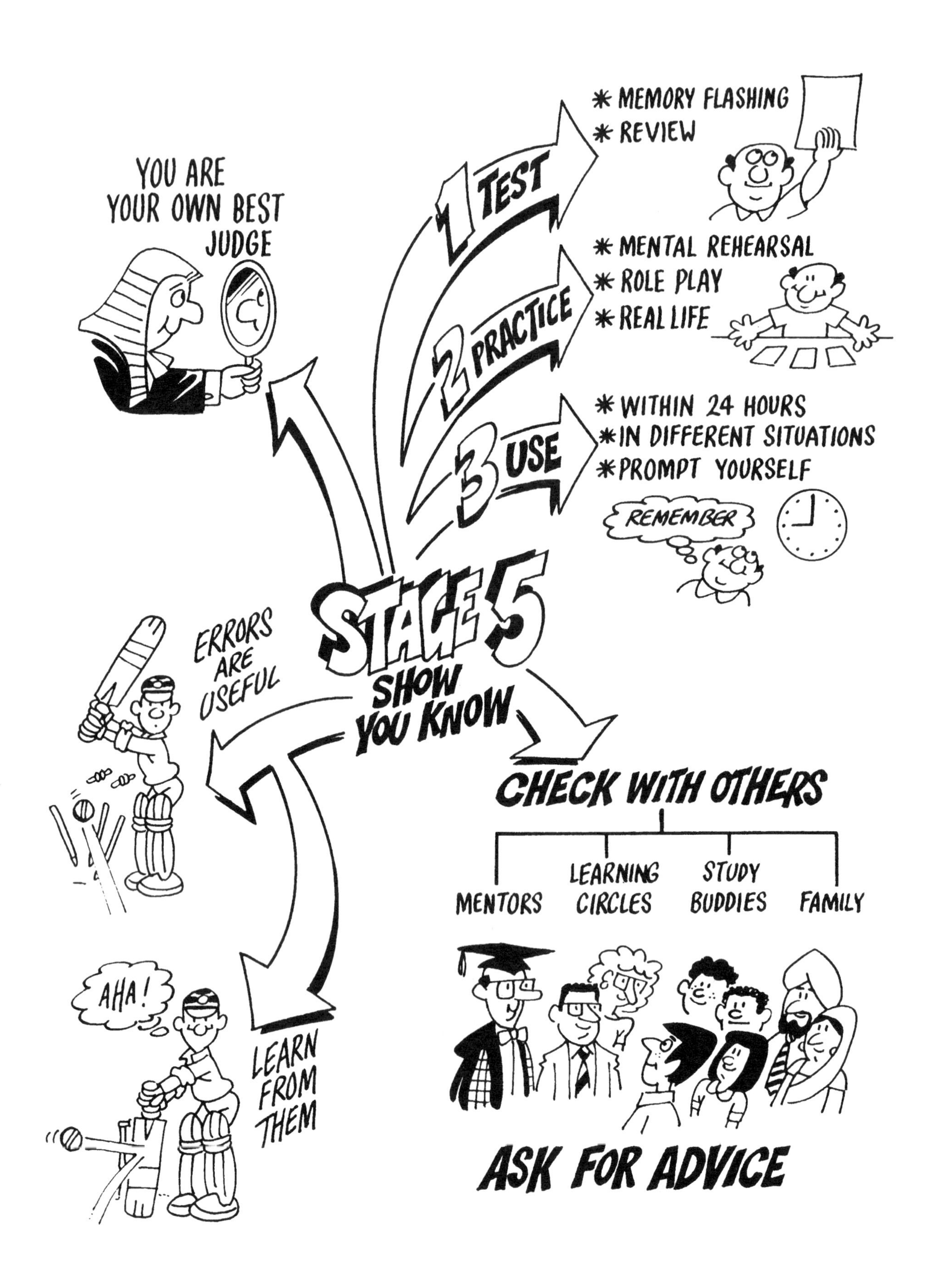

Check what you have learned about Stage Five

1. Who is the best person to judge your work?

2. How do you test yourself?

3. Why are errors helpful?

4. What do all top sportsmen use?

5. What skill do modern organisations value?

6. What is a mentor?

7. What qualities would you look for in a mentor?

Answers on page 216

A time for reflection

If you are a learner at work:

- The main ideas from this section that I will use in my job or career are:

  ____

  ____

- Although I originally did well in my studies, I can see that there are ideas here to learn even better in future. They are:

  ____

  ____

- I didn't achieve everything I could have done at school. But I could start to realise more of my true potential, if I:

  ____

  ____

- The following ideas will enable me to help the people I am responsible for:

  ____

  ____

- As a parent, the ideas that can help my children are:

  ____

  ____

If you are a student:

- The ideas I am going to use to help me learn more effectively are:

  ____

  ____

- Some of the ideas are worth talking over with my friends. They are:

  ____

  ____

- I really feel I would like to discuss some of these ideas with my teacher or tutor. They are:

  ____

  ____

Stage Six

Reflect on how you learned

Reflect On Your Learning

Throughout *Accelerate Your Learning* you have been frequently asked to think about the significance of what you have learned.

Reflecting on what you have learned is an important activity at **any** stage in learning. However, when you reach the point when you have actually used what you've learned in real situations, a period of quiet reflection is essential.

If you build up a **habit** of thinking through how things have gone, you will truly be in control of your own life.

Two simple but powerful questions to ask are:

What went well?	What could have gone better?
______________	______________
______________	______________

Keep asking those questions and you've learned the essence of self-assessment.

ACTION

Use the PERSONAL PROGRESS PLAN that follows to reflect on what you have learned through *Accelerate Your Learning*.

Notice it can be used, not just to reflect on this particular programme, but to reflect on **anything** in your life.

"Plans are only good intentions unless they immediately degenerate into hard work."

Peter Drucker

A PERSONAL PROGRESS PLAN

The most important things I learned are:

As a result I will do this/use the following ideas:

I can expect this initial difficulty– but I will overcome it by the following action:

I will check on my own progress. I will know I have succeeded when:

I will reward my own success by:

I need to learn more about this:

I will ask this person(s) to help:

The PERSONAL PROGRESS PLAN has some important features

- It allows for some difficulties as you actually use what you have learned. If you prepare for the ups and downs, then you will not be easily put off when you meet a difficulty.

  Stumbling blocks can be expected when you try something new. They are part of life and should be seen as helpful feedback not as destructive and negative events.

  You can turn stumbling blocks into stepping stones when you see them in this way. You learn to ask the all important question: "What can I learn from this, to be better next time?"

- It allows for self-assessment. **You** decide what you regard as success. ("I will know I have succeeded when . . .")

  This is an **essential** part of being responsible for your own learning.

  You can work out your own standards by asking yourself "What could I do if I was really competent at this?". That's the standard to aim for.

- It allows for rewards for success. Do you remember the importance of "Catching yourself doing it right"? You need to recognise and reward yourself for every success. Then learning becomes a pleasurable habit.

- It includes your future plans. Learning never stops. Each new piece of learning opens up other possibilities. When you review your own performance with this type of Personal Progress Plan, you are on the alert for new opportunities.

"In order to succeed, double your failure rate."

Thomas Watson
Founder of IBM

Only one creature ever sat down to succeed.

A chicken!

"A man grows tired by standing still."

Chinese proverb

Why using a Personal Progress Plan helps you so much

Author Stephen Covey suggests there are several characteristics of highly successful people. We would suggest that three characteristics stand out above all others.

"Good administration without vision is like straightening the deck chairs on the Titanic".

1. **They know how to make a clear vision of what success will be like.**

   That vision brings with it commitment, determination and a plan. You've learned that throughout *Accelerate Your Learning* – and via the Motivator Tape.

   In other words they:

   START WITH THE END IN MIND

"You cannot teach a man anything. You can only help him discover it within himself".

Galileo

2. **They take personal responsibility for all their actions.**

   You may not choose what happens to you – but you **always** have a choice of how you react.

   You can choose to be calm or to be angry.

   You can choose kindness over being hurtful.

   You can choose to be active or passive.

   You can choose to build your abilities or you can choose not to bother.

   In other words, they recognise:

   IF IT'S TO BE – IT'S UP TO ME

"I observed that nine out of ten things I did were failures. I didn't want to be a failure so I did ten times more work."

George Bernard Shaw

3. **They create the habit (it's not a natural gift!) of reflecting on what has happened or what they have done. Then they draw lessons for the future.**

   They learn from trial and error and they set their own standards. They measure their **own** performance.

   In other words they:

   LEARN FROM THEIR OWN MISTAKES

The last word (almost!)

On this learning journey, one thing has stood out. When we learn naturally and informally we do well. It's when we feel the pressure of formal or "study type" learning that problems can arise.

The answer then is to apply the sort of exploratory activities that you would naturally use in an informal situation to a formal learning situation. That's what the learning tools encourage you to do.

Look back at these tools now and see how often they reproduce the natural, unstressed way in which you know you learn well.

Look back, too, at pages 4 and 5 that summarised it all for you at the beginning of your Introductory Booklet. Doesn't it all make sense now? **That's because you discovered it all for yourself.**

Now, answer the **same** questionnaire as you did at the beginning. I suspect you will be pleased and surprised at the differences! The questionnaire, too, is a way to reflect on what you learned.

Finally, use the flow chart summary on pages 210 and 211 to create your own **personalised** yet systematic, plan of action.

Use this programme as a foundation stone for all your future progress.

In the final analysis, all great achievements have been accomplished by people acting on the conviction of their own vision.

Have you ever seen a park with a statue dedicated to a committee?

"They know enough who know how to learn."

Henry Adams
"The Education of Henry Adams"

"The only truly educated man is the man who has learned how to learn."

Arthur C Clarke

The End Of The Beginning

Fill in this closing questionnaire. When you have, compare your answers with the ones you gave when you started. You have, I am sure, significantly increased your optimism and appetite for learning.

Learning is a lifelong process. So this is not the end – it's just the end of the beginning!

Remember, for each question there is a "scale" provided. Ring the number that most nearly expresses your opinion.

	*NEVER * NOT AT ALL LIKE ME * TOTALLY DISAGREE		* AVERAGE		*ALWAYS * VERY LIKE ME * COMPLETELY AGREE
I am clear on the benefits of learning to learn.	1	2	3	4	5
I am confident of my ability to learn and enjoy it.	1	2	3	4	5
I realise that we all need different ways to learn.	1	2	3	4	5
I have clear goals for my life – at work/school	1	2	3	4	5
– in my private life.	1	2	3	4	5
I regularly think out plans to achieve my goals.	1	2	3	4	5
I list the important things I need to do each day/week.	1	2	3	4	5
I have all the capacity to be an excellent learner.	1	2	3	4	5
I believe that personal growth and learning never stop.	1	2	3	4	5
I know I am responsible for my own development.	1	2	3	4	5
I can study easily.	1	2	3	4	5
I find it easy to concentrate.	1	2	3	4	5
I can easily work out where to begin with a new subject.	1	2	3	4	5
I make sure I regularly stop to think about the subject.	1	2	3	4	5
I take notes while I'm reading or listening to a subject.	1	2	3	4	5

	* NEVER * NOT AT ALL LIKE ME * TOTALLY DISAGREE		* AVERAGE		* ALWAYS * VERY LIKE ME * COMPLETELY AGREE
I feel at ease with text books.	1	2	3	4	5
I flick through a book before I read it to get a general idea.	1	2	3	4	5
I ask myself questions as I read or listen.	1	2	3	4	5
I often stop to put what I'm learning into my own words.	1	2	3	4	5
I write down regularly the key points of what I am learning.	1	2	3	4	5
I use file cards or post card notes as reminders.	1	2	3	4	5
I constantly relate what I'm learning to my own life.	1	2	3	4	5
I often draw charts, pictures and diagrams as I learn.	1	2	3	4	5
I discuss regularly what I'm learning with friends or colleagues.	1	2	3	4	5
I often go back to my notes to remind myself.	1	2	3	4	5
I remember names and numbers easily.	1	2	3	4	5
I test myself on how well I know the subject.	1	2	3	4	5
I feel comfortable enlisting other people's help and advice	1	2	3	4	5
I regularly analyse how I have learned something so I can improve next time.	1	2	3	4	5
I feel comfortable using a library.	1	2	3	4	5

Pushing Your Comfort Zone

It's when you reach out and stretch yourself that you grow as a person.

One of the main messages from this course is that you learn well and easily when you **start** by playing to your strengths. However, you really start to "accelerate your learning" when you use all your senses and all your intelligences. In other words, your full potential.

If someone were to finish this programme and label himself or herself as "just a visual learner" or a person who "can only learn well if they can use their physical and inter-personal intelligence" – we will have failed.

When we put labels on ourselves, we start to restrict ourselves. We can cut ourselves off from new ideas, new methods and new subjects because they don't fit into our image of what we **think** we can do.

Reflect back over this programme. Were there sections that irritated you? Or made you impatient? Or some ideas that seemed against the way you like to work?

For example, were you a bit impatient with the section on goal setting? Did you find the background on the brain a bit irritating because it was "too theoretical"? Was the idea of concert reviews or role play strange? For some people the cartoons help make the point more memorable, for others they seem to detract from what they see as a "serious" subject.

Here is a suggestion. It may be the very ideas that initially feel uncomfortable that are precisely the ideas which – if you give them a proper try – will enable you to learn more thoroughly or to master a new subject. Or to become an all-round, versatile learner.

Someone who thinks the idea of goal setting is "too rigid and systematic for a free spirit like me" may in fact find that he eventually benefits most from planning his life a bit more.

In the same way, someone may initially react to the idea of backchecking their work for accuracy as being tedious. Yet, if she pushes through her "comfort" zone to consistently proof read her work, she is likely to find that her work becomes much more successful.

The techniques that initially seem the least comfortable, may be the very tools you need to use to ensure that you overcome potential "blind spots" and develop your full potential.

The following list invites you to consider how you may want to move towards the edge of **your** comfort zone. To push the boundaries of what you have done before.

If you feel comfortable doing this:		**You may need to stretch yourself to add this effective idea to your learning repertoire:**
Quietly reflecting, attending lectures, reading	• • • • • •	Active participation in cooperative groups, discussing issues.
Learning in groups, learning through games or role play.	• • • • • •	Spending time reflecting.
Making "to do" lists, flow charts, memorising facts, following a system.	• • • • • •	Using creative and learning maps and imagery.
Experimenting, building up concepts, brain-storming ideas, group discussion, putting things into your own words.	• • • • • •	Slowing down to be systematic and detailed and keeping to plans. Self analysis of your own learning methods.
Building up case histories, making comparisons, writing notes, using data bases or textbooks.	• • • • • •	Looking for unexpected connections. Using imagery or concert reviews.
Sharing ideas, pair learning, looking for the personal implications, concert reviews.	• • • • • •	Careful step-by-step analysis. Working systematically and independently.
Organising priority lists and sequences, practical trial and error, finding examples, making models.	• • • • • •	Considering theoretical background, using intuition, trying different ways of learning.
Visualising/imagery, using learning maps, diagrams, role play, seeing the big picture, using analogies, building concepts.	• • • • • •	Ensuring the detail is fully considered, weighing up pros and cons carefully, working to a systematic plan.

None of these ideas or techniques should be alternatives. They are **all** possibilities for **everyone** – it's just that some may feel more – or less– comfortable to you initially.

Success comes when you move the edge of your comfort zone and attempt something new and challenging. Meeting and overcoming challenges is what personal development is about.

Some of our happiest moments are when we stretch ourselves to reach new heights and develop new skills. Which would you enjoy more? To play a game you win easily, or to play a game you have to stretch every nerve to win?

If you become aware of your preferences and strengths and use them, you'll find learning is easier and faster. If you push to the edge of your comfort zone and build a wide range of learning techniques, including challenging ones, if you use the **whole** range of your intelligences, then you will have equipped yourself for lifelong learning and success.

You will have truly become an "Accelerated Learner"!

It takes courage to move from your comfort zone – but the rewards can be dazzling!

A Learning Map Of Stage Six

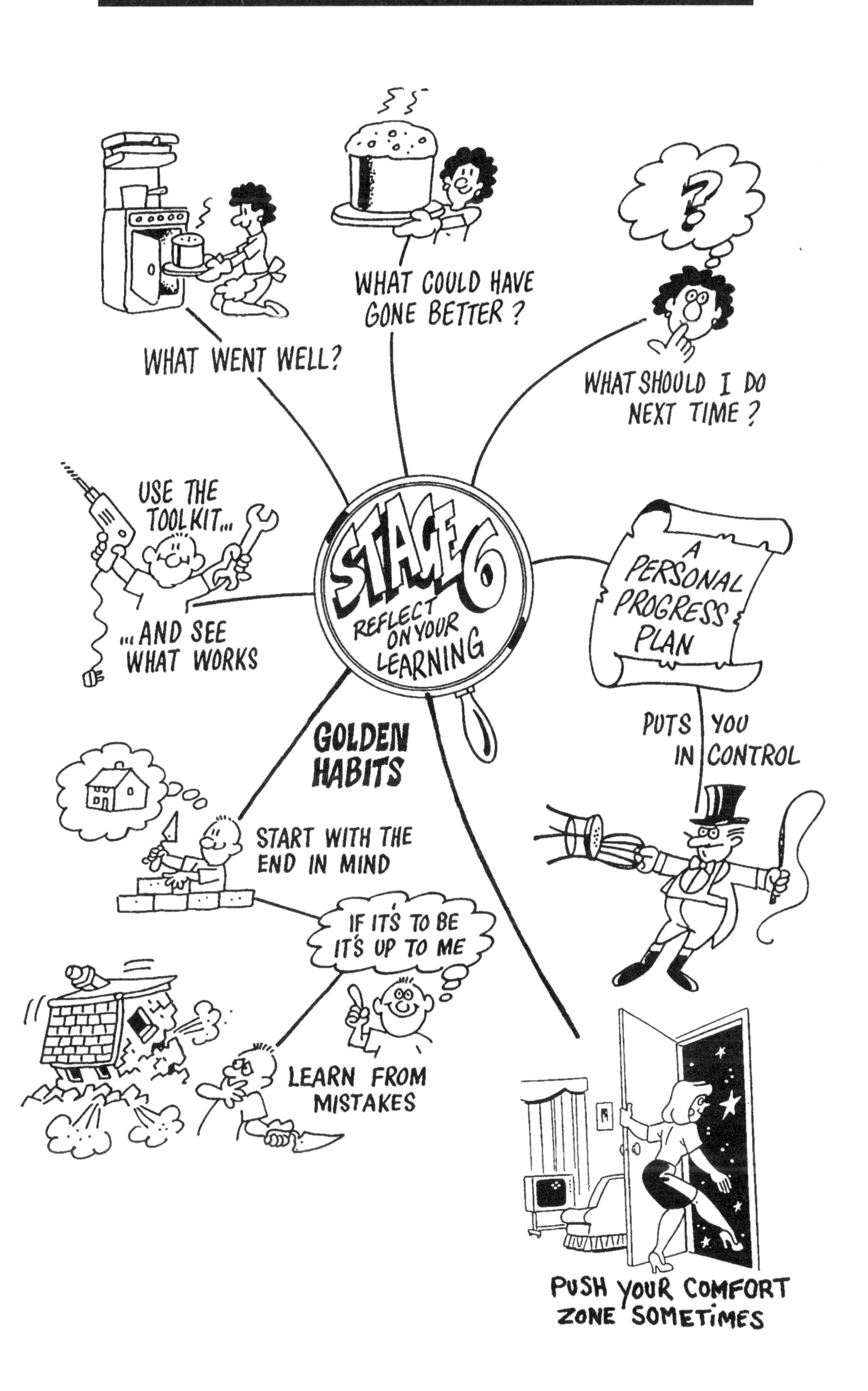

A Systematic Plan Of Action To Adapt . . .

Get into a resourceful state of mind	How? →
Scan read to get big picture	How? →
Sketch out what you know	How? →
Decide where to start	How? →
Form the questions you want answered	How? →
Adapt the material to better suit your sensory preferences	How? →
Explore the subject thoroughly through the range of your 7 intelligences	How? →
Memorise the key facts to trigger full recall	How? →
Show you know	How? →
Reflect on how you learned to improve your future performance	How? →

. . . To Your Own Preferred Learning Style

[Tick the techniques you intend to use]

Decide W11-FM ☐ Create a vision of success ☐ Write down your goals ☐ Create an action plan ☐
Plan your time ☐ Create a positive study environment ☐ Replay an image of past success ☐
Use affirmations ☐ **Relax**! ☐ Take frequent breaks ☐

Check the contents page/Subheads/Illustrations/Opening paragraphs ☐

Make a preliminary Learning Map ☐ Other form of notes ☐ Define what you **don't** know ☐

Start with the easiest section ☐ Start with most interesting part ☐

Turn every heading into a question ☐ Ask what does this **mean**? Do I agree? What can I conclude? ☐
Interrogate the author ☐ e.g. Does this make sense? What's the evidence for this?

V.
A.
P.

Highlight in colour ☐ Diagram ☐ Learning Map ☐ Visualise it ☐ Make a poster ☐
Read aloud dramatically ☐ Make an audio tape ☐ Explain it to someone else ☐
Write and circle key points ☐ Make notes on postcards ☐ Make a Model/Learning Map ☐

E X P L O R E

Discuss/Teach it to someone else. Compare notes ☐
Create a Learning Map or poster. Visualise it as a TV documentary ☐
Act it out/Role play/Model it/ Use postcards to order your thoughts ☐
List main points in logical order. Analyse it (A.E.I.O.U.) Create a flow chart ☐
Consider how this relates to what you already know and why it matters to you ☐
Summarise it in your own words ☐
Write a jingle song or rap. Play background (classical) music as you learn ☐

Create an inter-active image ☐ Create a mnemonic ☐ Memory Flash it ☐
Do a review concert ☐ Review the material on a **regular** basis ☐

Test yourself through learning maps or flash cards ☐ Practise through Role play or mental rehearsal ☐ Keep a learning log ☐

Use a Personal Progress Plan ☐ Push your comfort zone sometimes ☐ Create a learning action circle ☐

Some Issues You may Want To Consider

The aim of this programme is to accelerate **your** learning. But, in addition, the ideas that underlie the programme have social implications. You may wish to ponder on these following questions:

1. Has this programme changed any of your attitudes to learning? To education? To training? If so, how?

2. Is there anyone else you know who would benefit from the ideas and methods in this programme?

3. Have you discussed the programme with friends? Colleagues? Teachers? Trainers?

4. Should the way we teach and train be broadened to include these ideas? Would more people succeed if it was? Would more people enjoy learning if it was?

5. Do you believe that we often set our sights too low?

You will have gathered that we ourselves are not neutral about these questions. We believe that there is huge potential inside each one of us. We also believe that too many people fail in our current system and that need not be so.

If you have your own ideas, or would like to be kept up to date on Accelerated Learning, we would love to hear from you.

Suggested Answers

Introduction (p.25)

1. Because "academic type" learning involves things you need some training for – and we don't usually get it!
2. "Bodies".
3. Usually very helpful.
4. Because it ensures you get your thoughts straight and because it adds the extra element of sound.
5. "Believe". We act in ways that correspond to the image we have of ourselves. If we "see" ourselves as successful, we will act confidently.
6. Do something **extra** while you are learning.
7. Explore the subject.
8. a) Get into the right state of mind.

   b) Get the facts to suit yourself.

   c) Explore the subject.

   d) Memorise the key facts.

   e) Show you know.

   f) Reflect on how you learned.

Stage One (p.68)

1. **You** decide what is important. **Someone else** decides what is urgent.
2. a) Decide your goals.

   b) Create an Action Plan.

   c) Make a regular "To Do" list.
3. Your vision is your grand design for yourself. Your goals are more specific.
4. Willpower = Vision plus belief in yourself.
5. If your life is worth living, it is worth planning. Planning gives each of us a sense of purpose and direction and therefore commitment.
6. "Largely self-imposed".
7. An affirmation is a statement of what you will become, but expressed as if it was already true. It is deliberate, positive "programming".
8. Because we all have negative programmes that play in our heads and unnecessarily limit our belief in ourselves.
9. Reward.
10. When you are tense your brain operates less effectively and can even "go blank".

Stage Two (p.99)

1. Because it gives you a "feel" of the subject. You can sense where it is leading and therefore see where individual ideas "fit in".
2. a) It helps you realise you already have some knowledge, however small, to which you can connect the new ideas.

   b) It helps you define what you don't know!
3. Because you become involved and interested in finding out the answers. Your attention is therefore really focused on the subject.
4. Break it down into really small parts and master each small bit. Then move on.
5. Visual + Auditory + Physical. In other words, using as many senses as possible as you learn.
6. Use only key words and symbols. They unlock a lot of memory.
7. The information is on one page. It's visual and therefore easier to remember. You can easily see the connections between ideas. It helps you organise your thoughts.
8. Only what was **new** to you.
9. Because we remember twice as much of what we say as what we read. When you say it, you hear it as well as read it. So two senses are involved – sight **and** sound.

Stage Three (p.143)

1. Theoretical data is someone else's abstract idea. Knowledge is something that is meaningful and useful to you personally.
2. Linguistic, musical, bodily/physical, inter-personal, intra-personal, mathematical/logical, visual/spatial.
3. No.
4. When information is mainly presented to involve the linguistic and mathematical/logical intelligences, i.e. when education relies too much on textbooks and lectures.
5. By adding ways to learn that engage the other five intelligences, i.e. when you have the chance to use your full range of abilities.
6. By stopping regularly to think and explore what you are learning using your full range of intelligences.
7. Check back on the two "Intelligence wheels" on page 119 and 134.

Stage Four (p.179)

1. Repeat it or "activate" it. Do something to make it "stick".
2. Because it increases your recall of what you are studying.
3. Brief review brings the key issues to your attention and stores them in your long-term memory. It's important to review something you understand. Repeating things parrot fashion without understanding what they mean is a poor and usually useless strategy.
4. Make an **intention** to remember.
5. Research has shown that we do.
6. Studying your original notes or Learning Maps, putting them out of sight and then making copies until you can make a copy that includes everything on the original.
7. a) Split the word up into syllables. Spell out the letters of each syllable, then pronounce the syllable.

   b) Visualise each syllable written clearly in white chalk on a black blackboard.

   c) Write out the word, ideally in different colours.

Stage Five (p.195)

1. You.
2. Use the learning and memory tools you have acquired. Recreate Learning Maps, explain it to someone else, create a flow chart, create a list, etc.
3. They show you the stage you have reached and what needs more attention.
4. Mental rehearsal or imagery.
5. Informal teamwork.
6. An expert who will take you under his or her wing.
7. Skill in the subject. Someone who is informative, encouraging and supportive.

Suggested Reading

Adair, J. 1990. *The Art Of Creative Thinking.* Guildford. The Talbot Adair Press. ISBN 0-9511835-2-4.

Armstrong, T. (Ph.D.) 1987. *In Their Own Way.* Discovering and Encouraging Your Childs Personal Learning Style. L.A. Tarcher. ISBN 0-87477-446-2.

Baron, J. B.; and Sternberg, R. J., Edited 1987. *Teaching Thinking Skills.* Theory and Practice. N.Y. Freeman. ISBN 0-7167-1791-3 (Paperback) ISBN 0-7167-1789-1 (Hardback).

Blagg, N. 1991. *Can We Teach Intelligence?* A Comprehensive Evaluation of Feuerstein's Instrumental Enrichment Program. Hillsdale. Lawrence Erlbaum Associates. ISBN 0-8058-0793-4.

Bloom, B. S. Edited 1985. *Developing Talent In Young People.* N.Y. Ballantine. ISBN 0-345-31509-X (Paperback). ISBN 0-345-31951-6 (Hardback).

Borysenko, J. (Ph.D.) 1988. *Minding The Body, Mending The Mind.* London. Bantam. ISBN 0-553-17514-9.

Brewer, C.; and Campbell, D. G. 1991. *Rhythms Of Learning.* Creative Tools for Developing Lifelong Skills. Tucson. Zephyr Press. ISBN 0-913705-59-4.

Briggs, J. 1990. *Fire In The Crucible.* The Self-creation of Creativity and Genius. L.A. Tarcher. ISBN 0-87477-547-7.

Butcher, H. J.; General Editor., Edited by Gardiner, J. M. 1976. *Readings In Human Memory.* London. Methuen & Co. Ltd. ISBN 0-416-79220-0. ISBN 0-416-79210-3 (Hardback).

Buzan, T. Reprint 1989. *Harnessing The ParaBrain.* Cambridge. Colt Books. ISBN 0-905899-01-6.

Cameron-Bandler, L.; Gordon, D.; and Lebeau, M. 1985. *Know How.* Guided Programs for Inventing Your Own Best Future. San Rafael. FuturePace. ISBN 0-932573-00-2.

Costa, A. L.; and Lowery, L. F. 1989. *Techniques For Teaching Thinking.* Pacific Grove. Midwest Publications. ISBN 0-89455-379-8.

Costa, A. L. 1985. *Developing Minds.* Alexandria, VA: ASCD

Covey, S. R. 1989. *The 7 Habits of Highly Effective People.* N.Y. Simon & Schuster. ISBN 0-671-66398-4.

Csikszentmihalyi, M. 1990. *Flow.* The Psychology of Optimal Experience. N.Y. Harper & Row. ISBN 0-06-016253-8.

Diamond, M. C. 1988. *Enriching Heredity.* The Impact of the Environment on the Anatomy of the Brain. N.Y. Free Press. ISBN 0-02-907431-2.

Dickinson, D. Edited 1991. *Creating The Future.* Perspectives on Educational Change. Aston Clinton. Accelerated Learning Systems Ltd. ISBN 0-905553-32-2.

Ferguson, M., Adapted by Coleman, W.; and Perrin, P. 1990. *PragMagic.* From the Groundbreaking Brain/Mind Bulletin. N.Y. Pocket Books. ISBN 0-671-66824-2.

Flavell, J. H. 1985. *Cognitive Development.* Englewood Cliffs. Prentice-Hall. ISBN 0-13-139981-0.

Galyean, B. C. 1988. *Mind Sight.* Learning Through Imaging. Centre for Integrative Learning, 1442-A Walnut St., Ste. 317, Berkeley, CA 94709.

Gardner, H. 1982. *Art Mind And Brain.* A Cognitive Approach to Creativity. N.Y. Basic Books, Inc. ISBN 0-465-00445-8.

Gardner, H. 1985. *The Mind's New Science.* A History of the Cognitive Revolution. N.Y. Basic Books, Inc. ISBN 0-465-04635-5.

Gardner, H. 1985. *Frames Of Mind.* The Theory of Multiple Intelligences. N.Y. Basic Books, Inc. ISBN 0-465-02509-9.

Gazzaniga, M. S. 1988. *Mind Matters.* How Mind and Brain Interact to Create Our Conscious Lives. Boston. Houghton Mifflin. ISBN 0-395-50095-8.

Glasser, W. (M.D.) 1984. *Control Theory.* A New Explanation of How We Control Our Lives. N.Y. Harper and Row. ISBN 0-06-091292-8.

Glasser, W. (M.D.) 1990. *The Quality School.* Managing Students Without Coercion. N.Y. Harper & Row. ISBN 0-06-096513-4.

Handy, C. 1989. *The Age Of Unreason.* London. Century Hutchinson. ISBN 0-09-174088-6.

Healy, J. M. (Ph.D.) 1989. *Your Child's Growing Mind.* A Guide to Learning and Brain Development from Birth to Adolescence. N.Y. Doubleday Currency. ISBN 0-385-23150-4.

Houston, J. 1982. *The Possible Human.* A Course in Enhancing Your Physical, Mental, and Creative Abilities. L.A. Tarcher. ISBN 0-87477-218-4 (Paperback) ISBN 0-87477-219-2 (Hardback).

Johnson, D.; and Johnson, R. Brothers. 1990. *Learning Together and Alone.* Englewood Cliffs. Prentice-Hall. ISBN 013-528-6549.

Johnson, S. (M.D.); and Johnson, C. (M.Ed.) 1986. *The One Minute Teacher.* How to Teach Others to Teach Themselves. N.Y. Quill. ISBN 0-688-08249-1.

Kahn, N. B. Third Edition 1989. *More Learning In Less Time.* A Guide for Students and Professionals. Berkeley. Ten Speed Press. ISBN 0-89815-321-2.

Knowles, M. Fourth Edition, 1990. *The Adult Learner A Neglected Species.* Houston. Gulf Publishing Ltd. ISBN 0-87201-074-0.

Lewis, D. 1988. *Mind Skills.* Giving Your Child a Brighter Future. London. Grafton Books. ISBN 0-586-20034-7.

McNally, D. 1990. *Even Eagles Need A Push.* Learning to Soar in a Changing World. Eden Prairie. Transform Press. ISBN 0-9626921-0-7.

Machado, L. 1990. *The Brain Of The Brain.* The Key to the Mysteries of Man. Cidade do Cérebro. (Brain City Building) Rua Uruguai, 306 (esquina `com Gen. Espirito Santo Cardoso, 41) Cep 20510 – Tijuca, Rio De Janeiro, Brazil.

Maslow, A. H., Revised by Frager, R.; Fadiman, J.; McReynolds, C.; and Cox, R., Third Edition 1987. *Motivation and Personality.* N.Y. Harper & Row. ISBN 0-06-041987-3.

Meister-Vitale, B. 1986. *Unicorns Are Real.* A Right Brained Approach to Learning. N.Y. Warner Books. ISBN 0-446-32340-3.

Minsky, M. 1985, 1986. *The Society Of Mind.* N.Y. Simon & Schuster. ISBN 0-671-60740-5.

Obler, L. K.; and Fein, D., Edited 1988. *The Exceptional Brain.* Neuropsychology of Talent and Special Abilities. N.Y. The Guildford Press. ISBN 0-89862-701-X

Ornstein, R.; and Thompson, R. F. 1984 (Hrdbk) 1986 (Pbk). *The Amazing Brain.* Boston. Houghton Mifflin. ISBN 0-395-58572-4 (Paperback) ISBN 0-395-35486-2 (Hardback).

Parnes, S. 1981. *The Magic Of Your Mind.* N.Y. Bearly Ltd. ISBN 0-930222-05-9.

Perkins, D. N. 1981. *The Mind's Best Work.* Cambridge, Mass. Harvard University Press. ISBN 0-674-57624-1.

Rico, G. L. 1983. *Writing The Natural Way.* Using Right Brained Techniques to Release Your Expressive Powers. L.A. Tarcher ISBN 0-87477-236-2 (Paperback) ISBN 0-87477-186-2 (Hardback).

Rowntree, D. Reprinted 1989, 1990. *Learn How To Study.* A Guide for Students of all Ages. London. MacDonald Illustrated. ISBN 0-356-1533-1.

Samples, B. 1987. *OpenMind WholeMind.* Parenting and Teaching Tomorrow's Children Today. Rolling Hills Estates. Jalmar Press. ISBN 0-915190-45-1.

Senge, P. M. 1990. *The Fifth Discipline.* The Art and Practice of the Learning Organization. N.Y. Doubleday Currency. ISBN 0-385-26094-6.

Servan-Schreiber, J. L. 1989. *The Art Of Time.* London. Bloomsbury. ISBN 0-7475-0480-6.

Sizer, T. R. 1992. *Horace's School* . Redesigning the American High School. N.Y. Houghton & Mifflin Co. ISBN 0-395-57230-4.

Sternberg, R. J. Edited 1988. *The Nature Of Creativity.* Contempory Psychological Perspectives. Cambridge. Cambridge University Press. ISBN 0-521-33892-1.

Sternberg, R.J. 1988. *The Triarchic Mind.* A New Theory of Intelligence. N.Y. Viking Press.

Sternberg, R.J. 1986. *Applied Intelligence.* N.Y. Harcourt Brace Jovanovich.

Weinstein, C. E.; Goetz, E. T.; and Alexander, P. A., Edited 1988. *Learning And Study Strategies.* Issues in Assessment, Instruction, and Evaluation. San Diego. Academic Press, Inc. ISBN 0-12-742460-1.

Whimbey, A. and Lochhead, J. 1984. *Beyond Problem Solving and Comprehension.* Philadelphia. Franklin Institute Press.

William, L. V. 1986. *Teaching For The Two-Sided Mind.* A Guide to Right Brain/Left Brain Education. N.Y. Touchstone, Simon & Schuster. ISBN 0-671-62239-0.

Index

Q

R

S

T

V

W

Z